About This Book

This book may have more than you wanted to know about beer. On the other hand, it is the ideal handbook for the serious beer enthusiast. *The Essentials of Beer Style* is an unparalleled source of hard-to-find information about the process of brewing the world's great beer styles. As such, it is an indispensible reference tool for small brewers and for beer importers and distributors in their search for information on rare of obscure beer types.

The Essentials of Beer Style will also be an invaluable resource for aspiring brewers, students of brewing, and advanced homebrewers concerning the art of brewing.

For those who want to know more about beer tasting, the final third of the book is a full and complete handbook on that subject — a gold mine of information for aspiring beer judges.

If you really want to know more about beer, then this is *the* book for you.

● ● ●

THE ESSENTIALS OF BEER STYLE

The Essentials of Beer Style

A Catalog of Classic Beer Styles for Brewers & Beer Enthusiasts

by Fred Eckhardt

First printing September 1989
Second printing December 1990
ISBN 0-9606302-7-9

Editor: Jeff Frane
Cover Design: Charles Finkle, Merchant du Vin,
            Seattle WA
Illustration: J. Itsuo Takita
Typesetting and Design: Jeff Frane
Publisher: Fred Eckhardt Associates,
an All Brewers Information Service publication
ABIS, P.O. Box 546, Portland, OR 97207

Dedication: This book is dedicated to the memory of my dear mother, Amanda Regina Trapp-Whitney, 82, who was run down, June 5, 1986, by an automobile, in what became (5 days later) a crosswalk, in Everett, Washington. She was going to the store to get me a six-pack of Rainier Ale, while I cleaned the gutters of her garage.

TABLE OF CONTENTS

1

● ● ●

INTRODUCTION

by
Charlie Papazian, President,
Association of Brewers, Boulder CO

Sparkling, festive, strong, characterful, natural, original, estery, fermented, real, distinctive, hops, malt, yeast and water; if you were to take all of these and whirl them about like some mystical prehistoric soup and then electrify it with the spark of life you would embody the creation of Fred Eckhardt.

In the beginning there was Fred Eckhardt. Like no other beer author in America today, Fred's wit, savvy, research and knowledge have combined once again to offer the American beer community *The Essentials of Beer Style — A catalog of Classic Beer Styles for Brewers & Beer Enthusiasts.*

During the past few years we have witnessed the rapid development of interest in the appreciation of beer and beer styles. Let's face it, it is easy to fall in love with the taste of beer, especially with the excitement new American breweries have created.

Beer enthusiasts (I don't like the word connoisseur either, Fred) have evaluated beers for as long as beer has been made. We've been sniffing,

5

watching, "chewing," and listening to our beers for at least long enough to proclaim good or bad, gimme another, yes or no. But for most, it hasn't been easy to be able to tell whether a beer has less taste or is more filling.

Can you remember the first glass of beer you stared at, unknowingly wondering why; why the color was what it was, why the bubbles appeared as they did, why you liked it so much? In a sense it's kind of like the feeling most people may have when their automobile breaks down on a quiet country road; you pull over, get out of your car, take a few steps back in the warm sunshine, scratch your head and unknowingly wonder why?

For those who are car enthusiasts there are basic manuals, tools for the understanding of why things are the way they are. For the beer enthusiast there is Fred Eckhardt, his devotion to pioneering research and now a means by which we can help ourselves to understand beer and what it is.

Any good manual needs to make some assumptions and explain the groundwork from which it sprang. *The Essentials of Beer Style* does this with consideration to both beer enthusiasts and brewers. It is indeed a pleasure to be able to taste and evaluate beer with the help of a working manual of what's, why's, and how to's.

With Fred's honest and characterful style this book will be my drinking companion and guide for many a session, that is when I'm not in Portland, Oregon and happen to run into Fred, listening to his beer at one of the local beer estuaries.

Charlie Papazian
Boulder, Colorado, July 1988

● ● ●

FOREWORD

It's hard to explain this book. I'm not sure I wrote the thing, I think it just grew. First of all I was working on two other beer books: One about the beers by style, but more for the general public, and the other to be a completely new version of my *Treatise on Lager Beer*. Then, at the same time, I was planning to rework, along with my co-author, Jim Takita, our little booklet *Beer Tasting and Evaluation for the Amateur*. This book appeared instead of any of them. I'm not at all sure how that happened, but it did. I was trying to modify our list of beer categories, in the *Tasting* book, to conform to the breakdown used by Michael Jackson in his books. I incorporated some material I had written for a restaurant beer list, and the next thing I knew, and before I could prevent it, the main section (the Beer Catalog) of this book was taking shape, and it had a life of its own. Originally, I thought such a breakdown might be useful for the recipe section of the new *Treatise*. The categories grew from 12 to 20 to 30 to the present 38. As I was driven from one research effort to the next, the project came to dominate me, and occupy all of my time. My other efforts were stymied, and *Listen to Your Beer* publication came to a total standstill (that, at least, can be remedied).

I don't know that anyone has waited for this book with bated breath, but it seems to me that it will fill three important niches in beer literature:

1. For beer enthusiasts it will provide some mildly technical information about beer and brewing, especially in the contrast between what was and what is. The tasting section should educate beer enthusiasts in the taste elements of good beer, and alert them to possible defects as well.

2. For homebrewers it will provide information on what the famous beer styles of the world are all about, from both historical and practical standpoints. These initial guidelines should be helpful to brewing such styles at home, and a further introduction to the elements of beer evaluation.

3. For the new micro-brewing industry, I hope this will give enough practical information to begin the kind of research necessary to reproduce important world beer styles here in America, and indeed anywhere in the world. Micro-brewing is the coming revolution in the brewer's art, and it is spreading to many parts of the world, well beyond Britain, Belgium, West Germany and the U.S., where it has been re-born and is presently flourishing.

I feel that this information will be of value to professional brewers everywhere. There has never been an attempt by the brewing industry to assemble such a body, although Wahl-Henius in 1908, and Nugy in 1948 did provide information for brewers of those times to venture into some of the world's more famous beer styles.

THE THREE PARTS OF THIS BOOK

Part One is aimed at educating beer enthusiasts and homebrewers to some of the lightly technical aspects of beer and brewing, and to educate these two groups to the understanding of the Catalog of Beer styles that is Part Two.

Part Two, the Beer Catalog, is directed to the task of describing the great beer styles of the world, and providing profiles of beers within those styles, to acquaint the reader with what brewers of today and those of yesterday were doing within the described parameters.

Part Three, the Tasting section, has been done in cooperation with my associate Jim Takita, and is an update of our original work first published in 1977, and revised in 1980. An update is necessary, because since that time many homebrewers and professional brewers have begun comparative tasting of their brews. Guidelines for this type of tasting are not easy to find. The literature is scarce, and that which is available is aimed more at judging beer, than simple evaluation for the enjoyment and education of beer enthusiasts.

The two bibliographies in this book should be a great assist for those brewers wishing to investigate particular beer styles to a greater depth than that possible here. Bibliographic references in the text are designated by numbers in parenthesis, which refer to the reference in question. The bibliography is at the end of the book.

Fred Eckhardt
October 1988,
Portland, Oregon

● ● ●

ACKNOWLEDGEMENTS

I wish to thank all of the folks who took the time to comment and make suggestions on the various parts of this book. I am especially grateful to Jeff Frane for all his work and suggestions to improve the book and its format. Charlie Papazian of the Association of Brewers was kind enough to write an introduction; Charlie Finkel, President of Seattle's Merchant du Vin did the beautiful cover design; and Earl Van Engel of Portland's Blitz Weinhard Brewery took the time to read the manuscript and correct some of my technical errors, especially on the function of yeast. Kurt Widmer, Widmer Brewing, was especially helpful for assistance in translating information from German sources. Various members of Portland's homebrew club, the Oregon Brew Crew, were most helpful and assistance is also acknowledged from the following people (no particular order, but as they come to mind): George Fix, Tom Baune, Karl Ockert, Walter Scheurle, Vince Cottone, Paul Shipman, Jim Koch, Daniel Bradford, and especially Mike McMenamin; and indeed to all of the brewers, too numerous to mention here, who were kind enough to provide information on their brewing "secrets." Our profiles would not be possible if it were not for these folks sharing the kind of information which even a few years back would simply not have been made available to lay people under any circumstances. There just isn't room to list all of the people who gave of their time and energy to help me.

And I certainly would like to acknowledge the assistance of my co-author Jim Itsuo Takita, whose contributions in the Tasting section were most appreciated.

f.e.

CATALOGING BEER BY STYLE

CATALOGING BEER BY STYLE

Beer by the Style

Beer is found in most parts of the world, brewed by breweries in almost all civilized countries, and is widely accepted as a convivial drink, and as an appetite stimulant.

Beer is often thought of as a varietal beverage, wherein different types of beer are brewed in different parts of the world, and this is true to some extent. There is more to it than that, however, and an examination of various beers from various countries reveals that there is little stylistic difference between the beers of some countries, and great stylistic difference between beers within some other countries. Thus we find that the beer of the U.S. is very similar to that of Canada, Mexico, Australia, Japan and many other countries, while that of The Netherlands, Spain, Denmark and Austria is also of a similar vein; but that within Belgium itself, a country the size of Ohio, there is a huge diversity of beer styles — indeed, the Belgians claim a different beer for every day of the year!

It is clear then that stylistic differences among

beers is much more important than the differences between beers of different countries. We find, in fact, that beer is both varietal and seasonal, and that these varietal and seasonal differences are the most important aspect of beer appreciation for brewers, home brewers, and beer enthusiasts.

This little booklet is designed to explore the classic beer styles of the world. It is assumed that the reader has a familiarity with the process of brewing, and we have felt free to delve into the process along modestly technical lines, but if you do not have an understanding of the brewing process we can recommend the works of Michael Jackson (7b, 7c) in the references at the end of this chapter. Most of the other references on that list are of a more technical nature.

Elements of Beer Classification

Any beer, if it is to be properly evaluated, must first be grouped with similar beers. Beer is classified first by color: pale, amber or dark. The next classifier is strength, then method of ferment, and finally, traditional style definitions. We use all of those here, and others, too.

COLOR

Color is noted as pale or blonde, amber or copper, and copper or dark. There are necessarily some areas of overlap. American dark lagers and bock beers are usually thought of as dark, but many come within the range considered amber, if that were to be the only consideration. Many amber beers (i.e. "pale" ales) are downright dark in color. Some dark beers (i.e. some American darks) are definitely amber in color.

For this reason, our classifications are somewhat subjective in the matter of color.

COLOR DEFINITIONS

Color 1-10 scale:		SRM*
0	water	0
1-1.5	light straw	1-2.5
1.5-2	pale straw	2.5-3.5
2-3.5	dark straw	3.5-5.5
3.5-4.5	light amber	5.5-10
4.5-5.5	pale amber	10-18
5.5-6.5	dark amber or copper	18-26
6.5-8.5	very dark amber "dark"	26-40
8.5-10	"black"	40 & up

*SRM = Standard Research Method degree, roughly equivalent to the old lovibond degree, and is used by the ASBC, (American Society of Brewing Chemists). In this system color is noted as degree SRM. The Europeans use a unit called "EBC (European Brewery Congress) degree." This is variable, but sometimes:
1 degree EBC = 2.65 degree SRM, less 1.2.
1 degree SRM = 0.375 EBC degree, plus 0.46.

In our parameters we note color as 1-10/SRM*, e.g., **Budweiser**: 2 (1-10)/2.7 SRM. But sometimes, when quoting German sources, we also list the EBC color degree too.

So much for color, we just want to get you in the ballpark.

STRENGTH

The next classifier is strength as in original gravity (OG), apparent extract (AE) and alcohol content.

Original Gravity refers to the portion of dissolved solids present in the beer wort before it is set to ferment by the yeast. This is expressed in degrees Plato, which is equivalent to the total percentage of fermentable and unfermentable sugars. Original Gravity is also measured as the specific gravity of the wort. Either or both of these measurements is done by placing a hydrometer in the beer wort. A hydrometer (water measurer) is calibrated to note the relationship between the test liquid (beer wort) and water. This is called specific gravity.

Beer wort has fermentable and unfermentable sugars and some other solids dissolved in it, so it is heavier than water, which has a specific gravity of 1.000. Beer worts have specific gravities ranging from as low as 1.028 to has high as 1.130 in some very strong beers. The average table beer has a specific gravity of 1.044. Brewers refer to specific gravity as "gravity," but then they ignore the decimal. "Gravities" range from 1028 (sg 1.028) to 1044 (sg 1.044) to 1130 (sg 1.130). The British brewing industry uses the "gravity" system to describe their beer worts.

The U.S. and German brewing industries use the percentage of dissolved solids for their reference. These percentages are expressed as "degrees" Plato or Balling (named for their German originators, but Plato is the more accurate — he revised Balling's tables). The U.S. winemaking industry uses degrees Plato *but labels them* **Balling!** But that's a whole 'nother story.

There is a relationship between gravity (-1000) and percentage or degrees Plato. There is an average of about 4-gravity points to 1% or degree Plato (or Balling). Thus 1028 (1.028) -1000 = 28, divide by 4 = 28/4 = 7% or 7 Plato; 1044 (1.044)

-1000 = 44 = 11 Plato, and 1130 (1.130) -1000 = 130 = 32.5 Plato.

Actually the relationship is not exactly 4:1. It varies — 1028 really equals 7.066 Plato (and 6.984 Balling!) instead of 7.0, while 1044 is actually 10.96 (and not 11), and 1130 = 31.01 Plato. Nevertheless this rule-of-thumb is accurate enough for most purposes. When a hydrometer is designed to measure Plato degrees, it is called a saccharometer (sugar meter), and some hydrometers have both scales.

The Belgians use another scale related directly to the specific gravity. Here the gravity, less 1000, is then divided by 10, so that 1028 (28) becomes 2.8 degrees Belg, 1044 (44) becomes 4.4 Belg, and so on. Most of the world's brewers use one of the above systems. Some countries (e.g. England and Belgium) tax their beer on the original gravity.

METHOD OF FERMENT

There are many fermentation methods, but we generalize by recognizing just two. Warm and cold ferments are most often characterized by the yeast used in the ferment, and they are usually called top and bottom fermented beers. The progressive process of fermentation is called "attenuation" in the brewing industry. The degree of attenuation is an indication of how much of the fermentable (and un-fermentable) extract has actually been converted to alcohol.

Top fermenting yeast (*Saccharomyces cerevesiae*) is the original yeast type. It ferments throughout the body of the wort at warm temperatures over 58°F(14.5°C), and finally collects first at the top, and then settles to the bottom of the fermenting vessel. The yeast crop in top ferments is collected from the surface at the end of the ferment and before it settles, finally, to the bottom. The warmer ferment produces the more assertive taste profile we associate with ales. Top fermented beer is usually called "ale beer." Ale beer may be, and sometimes actually is, produced by a warm ferment with bottom yeast (see next). The temperature of ferment is a more important determination.

Bottom fermenting yeast (*S. cerevesiae uvarum*, formerly *S. cerevesiae carlsbergensis*) is able to continue working at colder temperatures. Normally, however, the ferment is carried out at warmer ranges, above 50-55°F(10-12.7°C). At the end of ferment this yeast settles to the bottom of the fermenting vessel, where it is sometimes collected for re-use. The cool ferment is often followed by a long and even colder aging period at temperatures down to 0°C. This type of beer is called "lager beer" from the German *lagern*, to store. As noted above, bottom yeast may be used in warm ferment to produce ale or what we call (here) "common beer."

To further confuse the situation, there are beers which are fermented warm, and then lagered cold as lager beers. Notably these are American lager-ales and German alts, although many other commercial ales are prepared in this manner, especially when the product is to be shipped abroad from the country of origin. Most notably this is true of English ale imports found in the U.S.

MATURATION AND AGING

Most people think beer is aged over a long period of time in the same manner of wine. Sometimes this is indeed the case, but most modern mass consumption beer is quickly made and quickly consumed. The most famous aged beer is "lager" beer. Lager beer originated in about the ninth century, when

Bavarian monks stored their beer in cool caves for summer consumption. They found that when they put ice in those caves in winter, the beer was better in the summer. The ice was harvested from nearby lakes and streams. This beer came to be called *lager beer*, and it was the lager beer brewers who first isolated the bottom or cold fermenting yeast. In those early times the beer was aged all winter, something like six months. The aging period served to allow a more complete ferment, with a less sweet final product. The aging period also allowed more of the insoluable fermentation by-products to settle out of the beer, resulting in a crystal clear final product.

Of course the same thing can happen to a warm (top) fermented beer, but the warmer temperatures hasten the clearing or aging process, so there is no need for a long aging period. Beer will mature twice as fast at $50°F/10°C$, as at $32°F/0°C$, and four times as fast at $68°F/20°C$. The more rapid changes at warmer temperatures give such beer a more pronounced, and less mellow, taste profile. These are the major difference between warm fermented ale beers and the cold fermented lager beers. There is one more factor, that of original extract, which must be considered. The higher gravity beers must be aged longer. And of course, it was only natural that ale beers would be aged cold (after a warm ferment) to improve their clarity and mellow out the taste profile.

Modern brewers are prone to substitute intense filtration for long aging. Modern lagers are often produced in 15-18 days time, and ales in 5-8 days. The big brewers are not always candid about these modern aging techniques, and they will still tell us about their long aging cycles. One mega-brewery even claims "beechwood" aging. This brings to mind huge beechwood vats, similar to the oak wine barrels which have made Bordeaux wines famous. Few modern breweries use wood vessels these days, and there are probably no beechwood vats anywhere in the world. Beechwood aging consists of adding beechwood slats and "krausen beer" to the beer after it has been aged in cold vessels. Krausening is a way of carbonating the beer through natural means rather than injecting CO_2 into the beer as is done in most breweries. This is itself a very classical method, because the beechwood slats act as a fining agent to settle the beer. The beechwood slats have an entirely different role than is imagined by most people who have heard of "beechwood aging." Some brewers have used this method of krausening with aluminum slats rather than the traditional beechwood slats. However, they do have the good sense not to call their beer "aluminum aged."

MALT, BEER, TASTE AND COLOR

The main ingredient in beer is malted barley. Barley (or any grain) is malted by first steeping the grains in water, and then allowing them to sprout, after which the sprouted grains are dried at various temperatures, depending on the type of malt and how much color and flavor is needed. The malting process activates the enzymes necessary to utilize the grain to make beer. Malted grains are easily stored, and are the primary ingredient in beer.

The brewer begins his work by adding warm water to the malted barley in a process called mashing. The grains' enzymes are thus reactivated, and they then change the starch in the grains to the fermentable (and unfermentable) sugars. This is the "wort," which is then boiled with hops to prepare the beer for ferment by yeast. The choice of malts and cereals in a beer determines the taste and color of the finished product.

Most American and European beers are very, very pale in color, and this is made possible by using malts which have been dried at very low temperatures, and thus impart little color to the finished product. Some American brewers desire an even paler product, so they use very pale colored 6-row barley malt as their main ingredient, and augment their beer with expensive 2-row barley malt and cereals — such as rice or corn — which add little or no color to the beer. American malt types were adopted from the Continental European malting systems, but with the changes necessary to manage the American-grown barleys.

American grown barley was found to be excessively high in protein content, while American six-row barley was also found to have extra enzymatic power. This allowed brewers to supplement expensive barley malt with less expensive corn and rice. That reduced the price of making beer by a significant margin. The extra enzyme power in 6-row barley was able to convert the starches in corn or rice to fermentable extract. American style adjunct-beer was born in the late 1870's, and American beer became even paler in color by this brewing innovation. Six-row barley came to dominate American brewing and the less enzymatic but more flavorful two-row barley was used in much lower quantities. Recently, since 1976, the 2-row variety has had a resurgence of use especially among small and micro-brewers. Premium American beers have nearly always incorporated a small portion of the 2-row malt.

British, and some Continental brewers, desire a

more deeply colored product. The British brew their bitter and pale ales with darker pale malts (normally from 2-row barley), and these are augmented by some malts which are kiln-dried (at malting) to higher temperatures. These higher kiln-dried malts add more color and flavor to the beer. Most important of the British style coloring malts are the crystal malts (Americans call them caramel malts). Crystal/caramel malt is dark in color from the caramelized sugars produced by the high temperature kilning which cures the malt to prepare it for brewing use. Crystal/caramel malt comes in many dark shades, such as 20, 40, 60, 80, or even higher, color degrees (as Lovibond degrees, similar to the SRM scale discussed earlier). American color malts differ from the European product, having much less effect on the beer's flavor.

German and Continental brewers use very pale colored malts, (Bohemian or Pilsen malt from 2-row Moravian barley) augmented by the darker caramel malts, but they also use Dortmund, Vienna, and Munich malts. These are similar to the Bohemian, but the end kiln-temperature at malting is higher, hence they have a deeper color. The Dortmund malts are similar in color to the Pilsen type, but the Vienna is darker, while the Munich-type of malt is the darkest of the three, and available in several shades of color as noted for the caramel/crystal malt types (above).

Most brewers make their dark beers by adding deeper-colored malts to their formula. British brewers use amber, brown and chocolate (from the color, not the taste), and black malt plus the crystal/caramel malts to color their beers, while the Continental brewers use darker Munich and caramel type malts, along with black malt, for their darker beers. Naturally these various malt styles add different taste nuances to the beer along with color. In general, the darker the malt, the less fermentable sugars are added to the final beer wort. The darker the beer, the more unfermentable sugars are incorporated into the final product (more on this aspect of the beer later). Some brewers have been known to fudge on their product by substituting caramalized sugar for dark malts in coloring their darker beers. American bock beer (III-2) brewers are notorious for this practice.

For black beers, (stouts and porters), brewers add unmalted dark roasted barley, along with pale, caramel, chocolate and black roasted malts. German brewers usually limit themselves to adding black roasted malts for really intensive color. And of course, brewers everywhere feel free to add whatever other ingredients as necessary to the product they wish to produce. English brewers, in particular, often add flaked barley, wheat, oats, or even rye (and sometimes malts from those cereals as well) to their beer, and of course they also use corn and rice, too. In addition to grains some brewers add white sugars (sucrose and/or dextrose), brown sugars, and various other fermentables such as honey, molasses and corn syrup.

German brewers have been pretty much limited (by law) to using variations of malted barley, only, in their beer (except for some styles, which are allowed wheat malt and barley malt). German, but not Bavarian, law allows much more leeway on the production of beers for export to other countries, and some brewers (**Beck's** for example) make special adjunct beers for export to this country.

Belgian brewers take great liberties in the brewing process by using all of the above, plus spices, herbs and fruits, too.

Originally (and traditionally) beer was "all-malt," that is made from only four ingredients: water, barley malt, hops and yeast. Other ingredients are used in various beer styles, as described above, and we will note them as necessary in this text. The malted barley is the primary ingredient in beer.

American brewers subscribe to both British and Continental brewing systems in making both ales and lagers, and thus incorporate any or all of the above into their beers. These days Americans are adding Belgian methods and ingredients to their beer as well.

THE UNFORGETABLE UNFERMENTABLES

It is especially important to know that beer gets much of its body and palatablity from the presence of unfermentable sugars called dextrins. The brewer manages their quantity during the mashing process, while he prepares the wort for boiling with the hops. Since these dextrins are so important, they too are a part of the strength measurement. If there is too much dextrin, the beer will be heavier, while too little causes the beer to be dry. Then there are times when not all of the fermentable sugars actually do ferment. The brewer controls this also. Crystal and caramel malts and special pale "dextrin" malts are designed to be less fermentable and to produce higher levels of dextrins in beer and these may be used with that objective in mind. Yeasts have varying alcohol tolerances, while fermentation temperatures have an effect which determines the residual sugar content of the beer. This can result in sweet tasting beer. The dissolved solids in finished beer are called "real extract" (RE).

Apparent Extract (or beer gravity) is another signatory in the strength definitions. Our discussion of extract has so far referred only to "original" gravity (OG), or that of the unfermented beer wort. After yeast is added, it attacks the sugars in the wort to produce alcohol and carbon dioxide in about equal parts, and some fermentation by-products. The carbon dioxide is discharged into the air above the ferment where it lingers, but the alcohol remains. Alcohol is much lighter than water with a specific gravity of 0.796. As the sugar is fermented, specific gravity is reduced in direct proportion BUT alcohol is added, and this lowers the specific gravity even more. There is a constant gravity drop during the ferment. Moreover, not all of the solids in beer wort are fermentable. The unfermentables are proteins, minerals, hop constituents, fermentation by-products, and unfermentable sugars.

But we don't remove the alcohol, do we? We need that in the finished beer, whose flavor is made up, by now, of water, fermentation by-products, fermentable and unfermentable sugars, alcohol, protein, minerals, hop compounds, and carbon dioxide. When we measure the gravity, or extract, of the finished beer, the alcohol changes the accuracy of the measurement of "real" extract. We call that reading apparent extract (AE) or beer gravity (BG). The apparent extract is noted in degrees Plato, the beer gravity in British gravity notation. This is simply the gravity of the finished beer, after it has had the CO_2 removed by shaking and agitation, and sometimes called terminal or final gravity.

Real extract is the percentage, degree, or gravity of the fermented beer after the alcohol is removed, i.e., the dissolved solids in the finished beer (as we noted above). Real extract may be measured by removing the alcohol from the beer, and measuring what remains with a hydrometer. Real extract may also be calculated (from the apparent extract):

RE = AE + (alcohol by weight x 0.46)

Thus, a beer with an apparent extract of 2.6, and 3.7% alcohol would have a real extract:

RE = 3.7 x 4.6 = 1.7 + 2.6 = 4.3.

Alcohol Content is the way most of us perceive the strength of beer, and is the one with which we are most familiar, as well as the one quality of the beer that is easiest to find. Brewers are usually not allowed to show the alcohol content of their beer on the label, but they will nearly always tell you what it is, or the wholesaler will usually pass this on. Most states keep careful track of alcohol content of all alcoholic beverages, and they too will pass this on to interested citizens.

The problem is that there are two ways of describing alcohol content, volume and weight. The by-weight (w/w) measurement, used in the U.S. brewing industry, is a comparison of the **weight** of alcohol with the weight of the entire amount of the beer. An alcohol content of 4% (wt) means that there are 4 grams of alcohol dissolved in 100 grams of the beer.

The by-volume (v/v) measurement is used by brewers in other countries and in the U.S. wine industry. An alcohol content of 4% (vol) means that there is 4% of a given volume (1-liter, 1-quart, 1-gallon, etc) of beer. Since alcohol weighs less than water, by a factor of 0.796, we can say that alcohol is only 79.6% of the weight of water. Therefore the weight figure is equal to 79.6% of the volume figure. A 4% alcohol content, by volume, is equal to 4 x 0.796 = 3.184% by weight.

Inversely, we must multiply that 4% by 1.256 times to find the volume equivalant: 4%/wt = 5.03%/vol. It is simpler to remember 0.8 and 1.25 for conversions. This also explains why Americans think foreign beers are stronger than their own. A Canadian or British beer of 5%/vol is the same as an American beer of 4%/wt. Most states have limits on the alcohol content of beer, reflecting on how it may be sold or advertised. Some states require special labeling and handling of these so-called "strong" beers.

There is a direct relationship between the (apparent) gravity drop during ferment and the alcohol content (by wt) which is 0.4167 for each degree Plato lost. Thus a drop of 9 degrees Plato would result in an alcohol content of 3.75% by weight. If you wish to determine the alcohol content, original gravity or apparent extract, you must know two of those three factors. For example if you know the alcohol content to be 4.9% by volume, change it to by weight (see earlier: 4.9 × 0.8 = 3.92% by weight). Now measure the actual specific gravity of the beer with a hydrometer. Just remember to warm the beer to room temperature, and de-gas it by decanting back and forth between two glasses or cups. When the beer has been de-gassed and is at room temperature (70°F/21.1°C) pour the de-gassed beer into the hydrometer jar, and measure its specific gravity. To find degrees Plato, divide the sg less 1.000 by 4. This will give you the apparent extract.

Suppose you find that the beer's gravity is 1.009. Subtract 1.000, and divide by 4 to find Plato. 1.009 -1.000 = 9/4 = 2.25 Plato. This is the apparent extract. To find the original gravity, simply divide the alcohol content (by wt) by the above alcohol factor of 0.4167. 3.9/.4167 = 9.36 (this is the gravity drop). Add the gravity drop to the apparent (beer's) extract to find the original gravity. 9.36 + 2.25 = 11.6 degrees Plato (translate to gravity, multiply by 4 and add 1000: 11.6 x 4 = 46.4 + 1000 = 1046 British original gravity (OG).

HOP CHARACTER

Hops are added to the beer wort while it is boiling in the brew "copper" or kettle. Hops are found in four forms. They are harvested and kiln-dried flowers or cones of the female plants. They may also be converted to pellets, where the essential elements (basically lupulin, where the important alpha-resin is found) are concentrated as powder, or rabbit-food-like pellets. The hops may also be extracted into a viscous syrup and added to the beer in that form, or the hop extract may also be pre-isomerized to allow incorporation into the beer at the very end of the ferment. Pre-isomerized hop extract is used in clear-glass-bottled beer, such as Millers, to aid in preservation and prevention of the light struck skunky flavor found in beer exposed to light. Such beer does have a longer shelf-life, but is still not immune to light damage, and lacks the fine hop essence and aroma found in high quality beer.

British hops are grown in hopyards with a few male plants (hops are dioceous – male and female), and therefore they have seeds. American hops also have some (but very few) seeds, and are considered "seedless." Continental European growers rigorously exclude male plants from hopyards, and their hops are truly "seedless." The presence or absence of seeds is an important factor in various brewing styles, and for that reason, are a factor in European Common Market politics, and a point of disagreement between England and Germany.

Bitterness in beer is produced by the amount of hops added to the beer during the kettle boil. Bitterness is measured in International bittering units (i.b.u.). The European Brewery Congress (EBC) and the American Society of Brewing Chemists (ASBC) seem to agree about this. Bittering units are determined by analyzing the beer, but generally speaking they are defined as mg/liter isohumulones, or parts per million (mg/liter) of the alpha acids of the hops.

A rough idea of i.b.u.'s may be formed, if you know the size of the brew, the amount of hops added, and their alpha acid content. The formula is i.b.u. = mg/liter of hops x alpha % x 25% (assumed utilization or isomerization rate). Bitterness estimates for the early beer analysis presented here were compiled, with this formula, based on popular usage of that era. These old analysis are mostly from Wahl-Henius 1908 *Handy Book of the American Brewing Industry* (15). Our original **Lowenbrau** profile dates back to 1867! We have also constructed several profiles from Richardson's old 1805 descriptions (10), based on our knowledge and his figures about wort and beer gravity, and hop use.

The full **bitterness formula** is presented here (1,4):

1. Determine the type of hops used, and their alpha acid content. Wahl (15) tells us that 1908 American (New York mostly) hops had 4.7% alpha acid content. We can assume that other standard hops used in Europe had about 75-80% the bitterness of their modern counterparts. German brewers used mostly Hallertauer or Hersbruck (5.5-6%), and Spalt or Tettnang (3.5-4%), while Austrian and Bohemian brewers used Saazer (4.8%) or Styrian Goldings (5-6%). English brewers used Fuggles (4.8%) and the famous East Kent Goldings at 5.6-6%.

2. Determine the volume of wort being produced (the quotes are usually in barrel figures, which need to be converted to liters). One English barrel is 36-Imperial gallons, or 43.2-US gallons, converted to liters, 163.66 liters. A hectoliter is 100 liters, or 26.4-US gallons. A US barrel is 31-US gallons, or 117.35 liters.

3. Find the grams (of hops) used per liter of wort. For example, Wahl (12) gives a one-barrel 31-gallon (117.35 liter) recipe for American bottled "export" class beer, calling for 12% extract (OG 1048), and 0.8 to 1.25-lb hops. Take an average at 1-lb, this is 454 grams of hops. Divide that by 117.35liter (1- bbl) to find the grams/liter.
   $454/117.35 = 3.87$ gm/l

4. Multiply this by alpha-resin to find total alpha acid possible in that wort.
   $3.87 \times 4.7\% = 0.182$ gm/liter

5. Multiply this by the "utilization rate." For the time being we'll assume 25% utilization.
   $0.182 \times 25\% = 0.0455$

6. Convert this figure (gm/l) to mg/l (or ppm): multiply by 1000 (mg in a liter).

0.0455 x 1000 = 45.5

The expected bitterness of that particular beer: 45.5 i.b.u.

Some factors can modify this figure significantly. The most important of these is utilization. Wahl (15) says "Hop resin is not readily soluble in water, more readily in saccharine (sugar) solutions, as beer wort. As the sugar is ...(fermented) the hop resin is gradually precipitated (from the solution)." Modern brewing scientists have determined that hops which have been boiled for over 45 minutes will have fullest utilization, that is about 28-30% between 45 minutes and an hour and fifteen minutes. (They also tell us that hops should never be boiled longer than an hour and a half.) Hops boiled for 15-30 minutes have an 8-12% utilization rate, while those boiled for less than 15 minutes or those added in the hop jack (hop strainer) or the hot wort tank, will have a 5% rate of utilization.

It was common British practice, in the early nineteenth century, to add all the hops at break (beginning of boil), and boil for one to two hours. In the late nineteenth century, they added half at break, and half after an hour of boiling (2-hour boil).

German and Continental practice included a two-and-a-half-hour boil, with half at break, and half after 1-hour's boil.

Americans added theirs half-quarter-quarter, at half hour intervals in a 2-hour boil.

In all three of those systems we can assume complete 30% utilization, nevertheless we have used the 25% figure as a conservative estimate.

By the end of the century, it was common U.S. practice to add one third at beginning of the boil,

boil an hour, add another third, and then to add the final third at the end of the boil or 15 minutes before that. That with a total hour-and-a-half boil. This would be 29%-8%-5% utilization, or an average of 14%. This is (roughly) the modern method used in many world breweries.

Late nineteenth century Europeans used a ½-¼-¼ system, with 17.75% utilization, and the English used ⅔-⅙-⅙ for their ales, (or other variations resulting in a 21.5% or 23.6% rate).

We have used all of these to speculate on bitterness of the old beers in our profiles. Those figures are just that: "speculation" or guesswork on our part.

BEER STYLES

Beer styles are the categorization of the various breakdowns above. Experts generally recognize about 30-styles of beer. Our system is based on that introduced by Michael Jackson in his books. We have stayed with Jackson because his is the best known. For that reason, this catalog is a little different than our first work, dating from before Jackson's *World Guide*. Further breakdowns have been stylized from separations by the bitterness level of the beer, as in the difference between American lager and International lager, or by the strength of the beer in question. We have designated 38 styles of beer in this catalog, plus another 42 sub-styles within those groups. These are arbitrary designations and, understandably, not all beer experts will agree with them. Indeed there are many who feel that top or bottom ferment should be the main criterion, and that has always been the traditional separation. On the other hand Jackson (7a,7b,7c) is the only other person to attempt the classification of all the beer styles in the world.

What we have done is to make those classifications, established by Jackson and others, a bit more specific, so as to be of use to brewers and beer enthusiasts everywhere.

THE BEER PROFILES

In the following catalog of beer styles, each has a set of parameters for the beer, and then we list a few beers followed by each beer's original gravity in degrees Plato (OP)/along with British gravity degrees (OG): the next figures are alcohol content by weight/and also by volume: after that the beer's apparent extract (AE) in degrees Plato/and the equivalent beer gravity (BG): and then the bitterness value in international bitterness units (ppm): followed by color 1-10 scale/and also (where available) the color in degrees SRM, this in a single line of figures for each beer. For example, this typical profile:

Budweiser

| 11.0/1044 | 3.7/4.7 | 2.1/1008 | 10.5 | 2/2.7 |

This table will explain:

beer's gravity OP/OG	alcohol ww/vv	beer's AE/BG	hops ibu	color/SRM
11.0/1044	3.7/4.7	2.1/1008	10.5	2/2.7

Translation: original gravity 11 Plato or gravity 1044: alcohol 3.7% by weight or 4.7% by volume: apparent extract 2.1 Plato or gravity 1008: bitterness 10.5 i.b.u.: color 2 (1-10) or 2.7SRM.

A fairly pale beer, with medium alcohol content; and somewhat sweet in taste, because of the sub-threshold hop level. (The threshold of taste for hop bitterness is about 8-12 international bitterness units). This beer is drinkable, but not especially noticeable. Incidentally, Bud has only recently reduced their bitterness. In 1985 it was 14.5, 38% higher than it is today (1987)! Now it is barely at threshold level. Brewers **DO** change their beer.

It should be noted that the beer **profiles** listed in the catalog were not chosen because we favored that particular beer, but solely because we had the necessary information on that beer, and for that reason only. This presented a severe limitation on which beers are "featured." As time goes by, we hope to obtain profiles on beers which are leaders in their class, for a more accurate picture of each particular beer-style. As noted earlier we required two of the three factors — original gravity, apparent extract, and alcohol percent, plus (if possible) the bitterness rating — to construct a profile for the beer.

This closer examination should result in acquainting the reader more intimately with each of the beer styles listed in the catalog. The reader should remember that these profiles are not etched in granite. Brewers do change their beer and its formulation.

We suggest that the color of the beer is a more important classifier than top or bottom ferment. This catalog is arranged accordingly:
1. Pale entries.
2. Amber entries.
3. Dark entries.
4. Wheat beers and miscellaneous entries.

The following are carefully presented standards showing what is expected, and traditional, about some beer styles. Some basics — *Regular Beer*: Original Gravity 10-12.5 Plato/1040-50 Gravity, resulting in alcohol of around 3-4% (w/w)/3.8-5%

(v/v), bitterness 12-35. *Special or Seasonal Beer, Ale, or Malt Liquor* — 12.5-14.9 Plato/1050-61 Gravity, 4-4.8% (w/w)/5-6% (v/v) alcohol, and 5-40 bitterness. *Strong Beer or Ale* — Original Gravity 15-17.9/1062-73 and 4.6-5.8/5.8-7.3% alcohol, bitterness 20-40. *Double Beer or Ale*, i.e., Barleywine or Doppelbocks — 18/1074 and up for 5.6/7% and over alcohol, bitterness 23-40. *Light Beer* — under 9/1036 and 3/4.2% alcohol, bitterness 8-20. German law defines *vollbier* ("full" beer) as 11-12/1044-48. *Vollbier* color is usually very pale 1.5-3/2.5-4.5 with 18-24 bitterness. It should be noted that "traditional" beer was "light" i.e., under 12/1048 and "heavy" over that.

These standards are rather arbitrary, and based on Continental usage from Narziss (9) and Jackson (7a,7b,7c) rather than UK usage (6,7a,7b,7c,14). We have relied on Wahl-Henius (15) for some turn-of-the-century American standards for English type ales, which is altogether fitting and proper, since the English tradition is about to be revitalized by what American brewers are doing, and also since they (the English) have, according to Protz (14), done what they could to destroy their own great tradition. This will have an effect, and is reflected here, in standards in the ale categories. Today it is becoming apparent that the British have no real standards, except those of the tax-man (14) who adds taxes for each increment of OG over 1030 (7.5 Plato). In any case, our basic brewing tradition is German with British overtones, and a touch of Belgian as well, an unseemly but eminently practical combination.

All of this is reflected in this attempt to set parameters in beer styles for a tradition embracing these many great and classic brewing traditions.

The separation of stout and porter, for example, or what is the difference between a barleywine and a doppelbock? How strong is a strong ale? We have answered many such questions here. We leave unanswered the question of what is amber, and how much wheat in a wheat beer? As to stout and porter, even though we have established parameters, we leave it to the brewer to decide in every case.

NOTES

● ● ●

REFERENCES

The beer specifications are from various sources. Jackson's books, my own inquiries, research by George Fix, and his associates in Arlington, TX, and beer parameter specifications gleaned from German publications, notably Professor Narziss' *Abriss der Bierbrauerei*, with translation assistance by Kurt Widmer and information about Pacific NW beers from Vince Cottone's *PNW Good Beer Guide* plus information and help from many brewers and breweries willing to share this intimate and previously secret information about their beers. Richardson's 6th edition, 1805 is quoted in Nithsdale and Monton (10).

BIBLIOGRAPHY OF SOURCE
REFERENCES –
BEERSTYLE PARAMETERS

(1) Bauer, Gary, "The Influences of raw materials on the production of all-grain beers," *Zymurgy Special issue 1986*, vol 8: no. 4; 9+, 1986: Boulder CO, Association of Brewers.

(2) Broderick, H.M., *The Practical Brewer*, 2nd Ed., 1977: Madison WI, Master Brewers Association of the Americas.

(3) Cottone, Vince, *Good Beer Guide – Breweries and Pubs of the Pacific Northwest*, 1986: Seattle WA Homestead Book Co.

(4) DeClerck, Jean De, *A Textbook of Brewing*. Volume One, transl., Barton-Wright, K., 1957: London, England, Chapman- Hall, Ltd.

(5) Fix, George, "Cereal grains: Barley, maize, rice and wheat," *Zymurgy Special Issue 1986*, vol 8: no. 4; p 20+, 1986: Boulder CO, Association of Brewers.

(6) Hough, J.S., Briggs, D.E., Stevens, R., Young, T.W., *Malting and Brewing Science*, vol 2, 1982: London, England, Chapman-Hall, Ltd.

(7a) Jackson, Michael, "Beer Styles: Creating Confusion or Distinction," *Beer and Brewing*, Vol. 6, pp 55-67, 1987: Boulder CO, Association of Brewers.

(7b)_____, *The Simon & Schuster Pocket Guide to Beer*, 1986: New York, Fireside Books, 1230 Avenue of the Americas.

(7c)_____, *The New World Guide to Beer*, 1988: Philadelphia PA, Running Press.

(8) Wolfgang Kunze, *Technologie Brauer und Maelzer*, 1977: Liepzig, DDR, VEB Fachbuchverlag.

(9) Narziss, Ludwig, *Abriss der Beierbrauerei* 4th Ed., 1980: Stuttgart, W.G., Ferdinand Enke Verlag.

(10) Nithsdale & Manton, *Practical Brewing*, 1947: London, Food and Trade Press. Quoting Richardson's 1805 work.

(11) Nowack, Carl A., *Modern Brewing*, (2nd Ed.) 1934: St.Louis, MO, privately published. Quoting Schoenfelds work on top fermented North German beers.

(12) Nugy, H.L., *The Brewer's Manual*, 1948: Bayonne NJ, privately published.

(13) Prechtl, Clement, "U.S. Specialty Malt Beverages," *MBAA Technical Quarterly*, vol 9: no. 4; 200+ , 1976 (presented in 1972).

(14) Protz, Roger, *Pulling a Fast One*, 1978: London, Pluto Press, ltd.

(15) Wahl, Robert, and Henius, Max, *American Handy Book of the Brewing, Malting and Auxiliary Trades*, Vol 2, Chicago 1908: Wahl Henius Inst.

● ● ●

*Additional bibliography, pp. 172-173

PART TWO
THE BEER CATALOGUE

THE BEER CATALOG —
THIRTY EIGHT STYLE DEFINITIONS

In this catalog of beer styles, there is a set of parameters for each style. These are followed by "profiles" of a few specific beers in each category with their original gravity as degrees Plato (OP) and British gravity degrees (OG); alcohol content wt/vol; AE Plato/AG gravity; bitterness; and color 1-10/SRM. For example:

Budweiser

11.0/1044	3.7/4.7	2.1/1008	10.5	2/2.7

Translation: original extract 11 Plato/or gravity 1044: alcohol 3.7% by weight/or 4.7% by volume: apparent extract 2.1 Plato/or gravity 1008: bitterness 10.5 b.u.: color 2 (1-10) or 2.7 SRM. A fairly pale beer, with medium alcohol content, somewhat sweet in taste, because of the sub-threshold hop level. Drinkable, but not especially noticeable. In short — a typical American beer.

This closer examination should result in acquainting the reader more intimately with each of the beer styles listed in the catalog. If the reader does not understand the above terms, please refer to previous section titled "Category Definitions."

COLOR DEFINITIONS

Color 1-10 scale:		SRM*
0	water	0
1-1.5	light straw	1-2.5
1.5-2	pale straw	2.5-3.5
2-3.5	dark straw	3.5-5.5
3.5-4.5	light amber	5.5-10
4.5-5.5	pale amber	10-18
5.5-6.5	dark amber or copper	18-26
6.5-8.5	very dark amber "dark"	26-40
8.5-10	"black"	40 & up

*SRM = Standard Research Method degree, roughly equivalent to the old lovibond degree, and is used by the ASBC, (American Society of Brewing Chemists). In this system color is noted as degree SRM. The Europeans use a unit called "EBC (European Brewery Congress) degree." This is variable, but sometimes:
1 degree EBC = 2.65 degree SRM, less 1.2.
1 degree SRM = 0.375 EBC degree, plus 0.46.

I. PALE BEER.
12 Categories — 101 profiles.
I-1. Pale and Amber Beer: Low Calorie (lc), Low Alcohol (la), Non-Alcohol (na), and Alcohol Free (af) Beer.

These beers may be of any color and fermenting style, but are usually pale (less than 2-3.5/ 1.8-4.5SRM) and bottom fermented. Low calorie beers (lc) generally have less taste, and medium alcohol (2.5-3.3/3.1-4.1%) while low alcohol (la) (less than 2/1.6%), non alcohol (na), and alcohol free beers may be more assertive, (but usually are not; except in the case of some European imports).

Non-alcohol beers (na) may have up to 0.5% alcohol (by wt). Many alcohol free (af) beers are brewed to have almost no alcohol, but there are probably no absolutely "alcohol free" beers. Some of the beers on this list are quite tasty, considering those limitations. American six-row barley malts and corn grits are the usual ingredients, along with Washington Cluster hops.

As for low-calorie beers, there's no way around the fact that alcohol contributes 7.1 calories per gram and there are absolute limits to what can be done. No one wants alcohol free beer if they are drinking to be drinking, so the beer must have a minimum alcohol content, and must be close to that of regular beer (as is the case with **Miller's Lite**). Everything else in production hinges around that fact. The beer can be made in only two ways: special enzymes to convert unfermentable dextrins (at 4.1 calories per gram) to fermentable sugars which will convert to alcohol. The other way is to add water. In fact that is what is often done. The secret ingredient of low calorie and low alcohol beers is: **WATER** — lots of it!

The apparent extract is usually very low in the case of low calorie beers (about 0.1-Plato/1000 or even negative values, i.e. lower than water as in **Miller Lite** and **Oly Gold**, which is indicative of the intense measures taken by some brewers to produce this beer style. The AE of low alcohol and non-alcohol beers is usually higher. Bitterness is usually under 20, but may be over that. OG around 7/1028.

A quick calorie count of any beer may be made by multiplying the original extract degrees Plato by a factor 13.5. Otherwise the container will (in the case of low calorie beers) usually state calories, along with grams of carbohydrate (4.1 cals/gm), grams of protein (5.65 cals/gram), and grams of fat (no fat in beer). If you add the calories from the list together, and subtract that from the total calories claimed for the beer, then you have the number of calories of the alcohol. There are 7.1 calories in each gram of alcohol, so divide the alcohol calories by 7.1 to find grams of alcohol. The label will also tell the metric weight (i.e. 12-oz bottle contains 3.55cl), so divide the grams of alcohol by 3.55 to find the alcohol percent by weight.

For example, the label on a bottle of **Bud Light** tells us it contains 108 calories, 9 grams carbohydrate, and 1.1 grams protein.

carbohydrate cals =   9x 4.1 = 37
protein cals   =   1.1 x 5.65 = 6.2
_____
total non alcohol cals   = 43.2
subtract from 108 calories   = 64.8
divide by 7.1   = 9.13 grams
                                    alcohol
divide by 3.55cl (12-oz)   = 2.57% by
          weight, which is 3.23% by volume.

the beer extract is 1.1gm protein + 9gm
                                    carbohydrate
                        = 10.1gm total
          non-fermentable extract in the beer
divide 10.1 by 3.55cl (12-oz) to
find the percent of extract:
                10.1/3.55 = 2.85% = 2.85
                    Plato = 1011 gravity

multiply alcohol pct (wt) by 2.4:
                2.4 x 2.57 = 6.17
this is the gravity drop during the ferment. Add this to the beer extract:

See changes for above calculations, page 185, Erratum.

$$6.17 + 2.85 = 9.02\% \text{ original}$$
gravity in degrees Plato,
which is 1036.1 original gravity.

The beer's profile, then is

9/1036   2.6/3.3   2.9/1011
est 10 bitterness| color 2

An almost tasteless example of the brewer's manufacture (certainly not brewer's art!), but one with more character (higher apparent extract, but less alcohol) than arch-rival **Millers Lite**.

PROFILES

beer's gravity OP/OG	alcohol ww/vv	beer's AE/BG	hops ibu	color/SRM
Bud Light				
9/1036	2.6/3.3	2.9/1011	n	2
Coors Light				
8.7/1035	3.5/4.4	0.3/1001	9	1.5/1.9
1985 original low alcohol LA **Grant's Celtic Ale Draught**				
8/1032	1.8/2.3	2.4/1009	39	7
Henry Weinhard Special Reserve Light				
9/1036	3/3.75	1.8/1007	16	2.5
Miller Lite				
7.8/1031	3.3/4.2	-0.4/0.998	19.5	2.5/3
Labatt's Light (Can)				
8.1/1032	3.3/4.1	0.3/1001	13	2/2.8
Michelob Light				
10.1/1040	3.3/4.1	2.4/1009	11.5	2/2.7
1980 **Oly Gold**				
8/1032	2.5/3.1	-0.8/0.996	10	2.5/3.6
1981 **Oly Gold LA**				
6/1023	2.4/3	0.2/1000.8	7	2.5/3.6
Stroh Light				
9.2/1037	3.4/4.3	0.9/1004	9	2/3.2
1967 original U.S. low calorie beer at 107 cals/12 oz bottle				
8.3/1033	3.7/4.6	-0/0.999	14	2/2.2

1971 German low carbohydrate beer (for diabetics-not low cal) 141 cals
   10.8/1043   4.3/5.3 0.51/1002   n   3/4.9
1971 Danish low calorie (81 cals)
    6.1/1024   1.8/2.3   1.7/1007 15.5   2.5/3.1

NOTES

I-2. Pale Beer: North American Standard, and Premium.

Very pale, cold fermented lager beers, medium alcohol content, (3.2-4/4-5%) lower taste profile, minimal hopping 9-17 b.u. (a little over threshold level), lacking in hop bouquet. Many Canadian, Australian, Mexican and other Pacific-rim beers are of this style.

There are often three levels of production in this beer style.

ECONOMY OR "3.2" BEER

Economy: These are lower priced and usually have lower alcohol content; indeed, some states (Utah, Colorado & others) have special laws for beer, allowing 3.2% beer greater availability in the marketplace. Typically, economy beer would be a "watered" version of the brewery's regular or standard product, see profile below. Little taste or character, despite the fact that there is a real need for a lower alcohol beer with a rewarding taste, as is found in some countries, notably England, where "mild" ales and "bitters" have a good following.

STANDARD DOMESTIC

Standard: usually this has a higher adjunct ratio, up to 65% in some cases, often lower gravity (11/1044 and less), fewer hops (not always), and mostly 6-row barley malt. There is often a slightly lower original gravity (10-11/1040-44), and slightly less alcohol (3.5-3.7/4.4-4.6). Although many "standards" are boring and quite undistinctive, there are good examples of this beer type, among them **Leinenkugel** from Wisconsin, and **Rainier** from Washington, both of which are clean and refreshing, as well as inexpensive. American six-row barley malt and corn grits, with Washington Cluster hops for bittering, and American Cascade or Willamette hops for aromatics are the usual ingredients in this style.

In 1977 the Master Brewer's of Association of America (MBAA)(2) defined the average and the normally accepted range for measurable parameters in U.S. lager beers as follows: OG: 11.4/1045.6 (range 10.7/1043-12.1/1048); alcohol: 3.7/4.65% (3.4/4.3-3.9/ 4.9%); AE: 2.5/1009.8 (2.0/1008-3.1/1012); bitterness: 16 (10-23); color: 3 degrees SRM = 6.75EBC (range 2.4-3.8SRM = 5.2-8.9EBC).

PREMIUM BEER

Premium: American breweries call their standard beers "premium," so these beers are called "super premiums" by their advertising departments. We will retain the "premium" designation, since there is absolutely nothing "super" about any beer in this class, no matter what the hype. **Premiums** usually have a lower adjunct ratio, 25-30%; often use a more expensive malt (some 2-row barley malt in the formula); and possibly rice instead of corn as adjunct. Occasionally a brewer will use more hops in his product: for example b.u. 16 instead of 14. There is often a slightly higher original gravity (12 instead of 11.5), slightly more alcohol (3.9 instead of 3.7), and richer apparent extract (2.6 instead of 2.1) all of which contribute to a more expensive product image reflected in the price. Sometimes color is deeper or paler, depending on the brewer's preference. Some of these are very fine beers, notably **Henry Weinhard's Private Reserve** and **Coors Herman Joseph**. For an interesting comparison, compare Millers U.S. **Lowenbrau** below, with the real thing, (see Bavarian Helles I-10).

Ordinarily this beer is made from a mixture of 6-row malt with some 2-row barley malt, Washington State Cluster hops for bittering, Cascades, Willamettes, and sometimes imported or US-grown Hallertauer, or Saaz hops for aromatics, plus corn and/or rice and medium hard water.

Common to *all* in this class: subtle to noticeable adjunct taste. Original gravity (OG) 9-12/1036-48. Alcohol 3-3.9/3.8-4.9%. Apparent extract (AE) 1.2-3.7/1005-15. Color 2-3.5/2-4.75 SRM.

PROFILES

beer's gravity OP/OG	alcohol ww/vv	beer's AE/BG	hops ibu	color/SRM
Bohemian Club "3.2"				
9.8/1039	3.2/4.0	2.3/1009	13.5	2/2.5
1981 **Budweiser**				
11/1044	3.7/4.6	2.1/1008	15	2/2.7
1987 **Budweiser**				
11/1044	3.7/4.7	2.1/1008	10.5	2/2.7
Coors				
11.0/1044	3.6/4.6	2.1/1008	14.5	2.5/2.3

1981 Coors "3.2"

9.9/1040	3.2/4.0	2.3/1009	13.8	2.5/2.6

Dixie

12/1048	3.6/4.5	3.4/1013	16	2.5

1981 Heileman's Old Style

11.3/1045	4.1/5.1	1.7/1007	9.3	2.5/2.7

1980 Henry Weinhard's Private Reserve

12/1048	3.7/4.6	3.0/1012	16	2.5

Labatt's Blue (Can)

11.4/1046	3.8/4.8	2.2/1009	13	2.5

Michelob

12.0/1048	3.8/4.8	2.8/1011	14	2.5/2.2

Miller

11.4/1046	3.8/4.7	2.4/1010	15.5	2.5

Miller's U.S. **Lowenbrau**

12/1048	3.9/4.9	2.6/1010	17	3

Molson Canadian

11.7/1047	4/5	2.1/1008	13	2.5

1981 Olympia

11.5/1046	3.6/4.5	3.1/1012	13.9	2.5/3.3

Pabst

11.9/1048	3.9/4.8	2.7/1011	13.5	2.5

Schlitz

10.8/1043	3.5/4.3	2.5/1010	11	2.5

Stroh

11.2/1045	3.6/4.5	2.6/1011	10.5	2

Superior (Mex)

10.9/1044	3.5/4.3	2.5/1010	17	2.5

Typical "3.2" beer

9.6/1038	3.2/4.0	1.9/1007	12.6	2/2.5

1896 average — 247 U.S.

12.9/1052	3.8/3.8	3.7/1015	28	n

1900 Canadian

12.1/1048	3.8/4.7	3/1012	32	n

1900 Mexican

12.5/1050	3.8/4.7	3.5/1014	32	n

1976 U.S. typical #1

10.6/1042	3.6/4.5	1.9/1008	21.1	3

1976 U.S. typical #2

11.6/1046	3.9/4.9	2.2/1009	21.7	3

beer's gravity OP/OG	alcohol ww/vv	beer's AE/BG	hops ibu	color/SRM
1975 average U.S.				
10.7/1043	3.5/4.4	2.3/1009	14	2/2.8
1975 average Canadian				
11.6/1046	3.9/4.8	2.2/1009	14.8	2.5/3.3
1977 American lager (6)				
11.5/1046	3.6/4.5	2.7/1010.5	18	n/2.45
1977 MBAA Standard (2)				
11.4/1045.6	3.7/4.65	2.5/1009.8	16	2.3

NOTES

I-3. Pale Beer: American All-Malt Lagers.

These are very pale, cold fermented lager beers, with medium alcohol content, (3.5-4/4.5-5%), lower taste profile, minimal hopping, 14-19 b.u., and lacking in hop bouquet. Some American all-malt lagers (more assertive) are listed later (I-6). Extract 11-12.5/1044-50. Apparent extract 2.2-3.7/1009-15. Color 2- 3.5/2.5-4.5. This style is intended to match premium American beer in its taste profile, and differs from the new American Pilsner style lager (I-6) only in that beer's higher hop rate (19-35 bu, as opposed to the lower 14-18 rate quoted above). Ingredients are similar to those of American Premium (I-2), but will have no grain (corn or rice) adjuncts.

PROFILES

beer's gravity OP/OG	alcohol ww/vv	beer's AE/BG	hops ibu	color/SRM
Island Pacific Goldstream Lager (Can)				
9.5/1038	3.1/3.9	2/1008	14	3
Okanagan Spring Premium Lager (Can)				
12.2/1049	4/5	2.6/1010	17	2.5/n
Smith & Reilly Honest Beer				
11.9/1048	3.8/4.8	2.75/1011	18	3.5/10

NOTES

I-4. Pale Beer: American Sparkling Lager Ale

Sparkling ale originated in the late nineteenth century as a lagered, and bottled, ale version of the very pale Bohemian lager beer. Today the beverage which was originally called "sparkling ale" is not found as such, but is labeled as, and called, either **American Ale** or **cream ale**: i.e., very pale, warm (bottom or top) fermented beer, which is cold lagered as lager beer. The term "cream ale" is often used instead of "sparkling ale" as a name for this category. This is an incorrect use of that name because, originally "cream ale" was the beer we (here) call blonde or golden *draft* ale. These are now brewed by the new micros, and served direct or bottled direct, filtered but without aging, in a manner very close to the classic "cream ale" tradition of the late nineteenth century.

Alcohol content of American sparkling lager-ale is medium, (3.5-4.5/4.4-5.6%), and parameters are almost identical to to that of the standard American lager: minimal taste profile, minimal hopping, and lacking in hop bouquet. This style, when brewed with bottom yeast (common), is called "bastard ale" in old brewing literature, an apt title. Nevertheless, there are a few fairly good examples of this type with modest hop levels, and certainly with more taste than the American standard. In general this beer will be less boring than American standard or even premium lager.

Some beer writers and new brewers are scornful of this style because many examples are bottom fermented, but no matter the yeast, the warm ferment followed by lagering is a distinctive American contribution to brewing science and the name *American Ale* is quite fitting and proper, since the technical term "ale" has long been defined (in

American brewing literature) as more pertinent to the brewing temperature than to the choice of yeast. Some of these beers are combinations of top and bottom fermented brews. That is, brewed as top fermented ale, but then krausened with lager wort and yeast. Krausening is a process where the beer, after ferment and aging, has a "dosage" added. This is a method similar to that used in the Champagne charmot process, where sugar and yeast are added in a special tank, starting a second ferment, and charging the liquor with carbon dioxide. In this case the "dosage" is "krausen beer," fresh, newly fermenting lager beer wort. Traditionally, this beer-type had an original extract over 13/1052, but today we find OE from 11-14/1044-56, apparent extract 1.7-2.8/1007-1012, bitterness 10-22, and color 2.5-3.5/2.0-4.4SRM. Ingredients used are similar to American premiums (I-2) but dextrose (corn sugar) or corn syrup is also used by some brewers of this beer-type. See also Blonde or Golden ales (I-12) for a similar, yet quite different brew.

EUROPEAN SPARKLING LAGER ALES

These are closely related to American ales, that is, they are warm (top) fermented, cold lagered beers. The significant difference is hop rates. European ales are very similar in taste to Euro-lagers, and are more likely to be all-malt than their American counterparts, as **Sezoens**, our only current profile shows. Original extract 11-14.9/1044-1062. Apparent extract 2-4/1008-1016. Alcohol 3.5-4.5/4.4-5.6%. Bitterness 20-40. Color 2-3.5/2-4.4SRM. These would be formulated similarly to International lagers (see I-7).

PROFILES

beer's gravity OP/OG	alcohol ww/vv	beer's AE/BG	hops ibu	color/SRM
1946 Black Horse Ale				
11.6/1046	3.9/4.9	2.3/1009	n	4.0/6.5
1946 Carling Red Cap Ale				
12/1048	3.8/4.9	2.7/1011	n	3.5/5.25
Labatt's 50 Ale (Can)				
11.6/1046	3.9/4.9	2.1/1008	14	2.5
Molson Ale (Can)				
11.7/1047	3.9/4.9	1009	14.5	2.5
Sezoen Belgian Ale				
12/1048	4.2/5.4	1.9/1008	n	3
Weinhard's Light American Ale				
12/1048	3.9/4.9	2.9/1012	15	3
1901 American sparkling ale				
13.9/1057	4.9/6.2	2.1/1009	60	n
1975 average U.S.				
11.9/1048	3.8/4.8	2.8/1011	12.5	3/4.3
1975 average Canadian				
11.4/1045	3.9/4.8	2.1/1008	16	3/4.1

NOTES

I-5. Pale Beer: American Malt Liquors and Japanese Dry Beer

AMERICAN MALT LIQUORS

Very pale, cold fermented lager beers, strong alcohol content, (except in 3.2% states, where they will have only 3.2/4% alcohol, which is a blatant misrepresentation of style) of up to 6.5/8.1%, or possibly even higher. By definition this beer style has minimal taste profile, minimal hopping, lacking in hop bouquet and threshold hop levels, (bitterness 5-14). They are described by Prechtl (13) as "...estery, vinous and lightly hopped, higher in alcohol (4.5-5.5/5.6-6.9%), (and) original extract 12.5-14.5/1050-59." He describes the manufacture as an increase of the gravity of normal wort with dextrose (corn) sugar or syrup, or alternately as a special brew with 50-60% malt, 30-40% corn grits, plus 10-20% dextrose. Normal mash procedure, but conversion in the 140-150°F (60-66°C) range. Cluster hops at 12-14 or lower bitterness.

Originally, a fungal enzyme, such as *Aspergillus oryzae*, was added to convert the unfermentable dextrins in the beer to fermentable sugars, thus increasing the alcohol, and decrease the apparent or beer extract, in the finished product. More recently, brewers have taken to using genetically engineered yeast strains (see Dry Beer, below) for the same effect. Through these procedures, malt liquors have less body, but more alcohol, than their "ordinary" counterparts. They are fermented with lager yeast, but at ale or warm temperatures for 6-8 days. Terminal extract (apparent extract) is 0.7-2.7/1003-1011, or even lower. The yeast is discarded, because this type of ferment ruins the stuff! The beer is lagered for 1-5 weeks at

32°F(0°C), and processed as lager beer. From time to time this beer has been processed as citrus flavored malt liquor (see IV-6).

What the American brewing industry is really saying, with this category, is that these beers are "different," with the implicit promise of higher, cheaper alcohol content. They are often heavily advertised in poor, urban black communities, perhaps with that assumption. They are best consumed very cold (32-36°F/0-2.5°C), since there is so little taste to them. The taste is insipid, because the flavor profile is so low. There are few recommended beers in this category. The Stroh Brewing Company's **Schlitz Red Bull** is a sterling example as to why this is so. The alcohol content was raised from a reasonable 4.5%/5.7% in the **Blue Bull** to a new low in highs at 5.5%/6.9%. All they changed was the alcohol content; the beer is still as insipid as ever. "Bull" is the proper name for such a beer. This type has an original gravity of 12-16/1048-64 and higher. Apparent extract 1.1-2.8/1004-12. Color is usually very pale: 1.5-3.5/1-4SRM. Bitterness, as noted above, the bare minimum to allow the beverage to be called a malt beverage under the law.

JAPANESE DRY BEER

This is a more acceptable beer, a well-balanced, although "engineered" beer type. Closely related to malt liquors (above), dry beer was introduced by the **Asahi Brewing Company** of Tokyo, Japan, in February 1987. **Asahi Super Dry** became so popular that year that it was quickly copied by other Japanese brewers. Recently, during the latter half of 1988, it was introduced to the U.S. market. "Dry" means not so sweet, and dry beer is basically a lower alcohol-content malt liquor, where the beer is force fermented to reduce the final gravity, by using special genetic engineering techniques to produce a yeast strain with a built-in dextrin hydrolizing enzyme to change the normally unfermentable dextrins into fermentable sugars. The alcohol content of the final product is usually kept at, or just above that of regular beer (4-5%). The original gravity is adjusted, accordingly, to something around 10.5/1042. A bitterness level of 15-23 seems likely, since the lower level of sweetness would enhance existing hop elements. Color is within the normal pale lager range. The beer gravity is necessarily low in the 0.8-1.4/1003-1005 range, depending on OG.

The major Japanese breweries (**Sapporo**, **Kirin**, **Asahi** and **Suntory**) have each produced examples of this beer type, and as we go to print, **Heileman** and **Anheuser-Busch** are test marketing their **Heileman Old Style Dry** and **Michelob Dry**, while **Miller** is doing additional research.

A reduction in sweetness is a very appealing characteristic in a table beer, making it more compatible with fine dining. Dry beer seems to fill a niche as a table beer at quality establishments, meeting an important need in dining. Dry beer goes especially well with broiled or steamed fish dishes, and is eminently suited to the nouveau European cuisine, with its lower fat levels, and is especially good with Japanese or Chinese food. It is less satisfactory with hot dishes such as Szechuan, Korean, Thai, Mexican or Cajun cuisine. It is also less suitable to accompany traditional beer food, i.e., sausage, fatty meats and such. It has the further advantage of having 8.5% fewer calories than regular beer.

PROFILES

beer's gravity OP/OG	alcohol ww/vv	beer's AE/BG	hops ibu	color/SRM
1946 Champale ML				
12.3/1049	4.4/5.6	1.7/1007	5	1.5/1
1976 Colt 45 ML				
11.3/1045	4.2/5.3	1.1/1004	7	2.5/3.1
1987 Colt 45 ML				
14/1057	5/6.3	2/1008	15	2.5/3.5
Labatt's Extra Stock ML (Can)				
13.6/1054	3.9/4.9	4.1/1016	22.5	2.5/n
1980 Mickey's Big Mouth				
12/1048	4.4/5.5	1.8/1007	15	3/2.5
1980 Old English 800 ML				
17/1070	6.6/8.3	1.6/1006	15	3.7/3.5
1941 Skyball ML (prototype ML)				
11.9/1047	4.7/5.9	0.56/1002	14	n/3.25
1970 U.S.ML #1				
12.5/1050	4.7/5.9	1.26/1005	13	n/3.1
1970 U.S.ML #2				
13.5/1055	5.4/6.7	0.85/1003	12.5	n/3.1
1988 average 2 Japanese dry beers				
10.4/1042	3.99/5.01	1/1004	est 18	n/2.5

NOTES

I-6. Pale Beer: New American Pilsen-Style Lager.

Very pale beer, medium alcohol (3.5-4/4.5-5%), mild to richly assertive profile, noticeable to moderate, or even impressive hoppiness, and with some hop bouquet. These all should be *all-malt beers*. Some call these "American Pilsners," but they may be quite different from that style because of malt and hop differences in the American product. Original gravity 10.9-12.9/1044-1051. Apparent extract 2.2-4.2/1009-1017. Bitterness 20-40. Color 2-3.5/2.5-4.5SRM. Ingredients used are similar to the those in American all-malt (I-3) and American premium (I-2); but without the adjuncts, of course, and more hops, especially aromatic hops, such as Perle, Hallertauer, Saaz, Northern Brewer, either imported or American.

PROFILES

beer's gravity OP/OG	alcohol ww/vv	beer's AE/BG	hops ibu	color/SRM
August Schell Pilsner				
12.5/1050	4/5	2.7/1011	n	3.5
Island Lager (Can)				
11.8/1047	4/5	2.2/1009	25	3.5
Samuel Adams Boston Lager				
12.5/1050	3.5/4.4	4.2/1017	35	3

NOTES

I-7. Pale Beer: International Style Lagers

These are very pale beers with medium alcohol
(3.5-4.5/4.4-5.7%) mild to richly assertive taste
profile, noticeable to moderate, or even impressive
hoppiness, and usually with some hop bouquet. We
believe these should be *all-malt beers*, but of course
that is not often the case. Some are labeled "Malt
Liquor" (strong beer — over 4/5%). Original extract 10-13/1040-52. Apparent extract 2.2-3.7/
1009-1015. Bitterness 18-30. Color 2-3.5/2.5-4.5
SRM. Some are ordinary "American" with a few
more hops thrown in to hide the corn (**Becks**).
(Compare **Becks** West Germany brew next (I-8). Ingredients: pale two-row European barley malt, and
perhaps a minimal grain adjunct of not more than
25% rice or corn. Continental hops are
used — Hallertauer, Northern Brewer, Saaz, Tettnang, Spalt or Perle; and medium hard water to
400ppm maximum.

British lagers, at least those in England, will
often be of abysmally low gravity, and this may ac-
count for the apathy towards lagers found in that
country, because the English version is pretty
pathetic compared with European beers as found in
Europe, or even as found in this country. Hough *et
al* (6) gives us some findings about British lagers in
1960: extract 7.4-9.1 /1030-36; alcohol 2.6-2.9/
3.3-3.6%; but better in bitterness at 20-32. In this
country such beers would certainly find little accep-
tance.

Almost every country in the world (at least those
which allow or have breweries) brews this beer, but
if the hop level is below 20 i.b.u., we have chosen to
catalog the type as "American Premium."

PROFILES

beer's gravity OP/OG	alcohol ww/vv	beer's AE/BG	hops ibu	color/SRM
Becks (WG-for export only)				
11/1044	3.7/4.6	3.1/1012	23	2/2.5
1907 **Carlsberg Lager** (Den)				
13.9/1057	4.3/5.4	3.6/1014	40	n
Carlsberg Lager (Den)				
10.9/1044	3.8/4.8	1.8/1007	23	2.5
Harp Lager (Ir)				
11.1/1044	3.6/4.5	3.2/1013	24.5	2/2.7
Heineken (Neth)				
12.2/1049	4/5.2	2.7/1011	18	2.5/4.3
1907 **Kirin Lager** (Japan)				
13.1/1053	4.0/5.0	3.4/1013	40	n
Lowenbrau Zurich (Swiss)				
11.5/1046	3.9/4.9	2.1/1008	n	2.5
Ringnes (Nor)				
12.9/1052	4.3/5.4	3.7/1015	27	3.5/5.5
Steffl Pils (Austria)				
12.5/1050	4/5	3/1012	35	3.5
1984 Swiss Brewing Institute Standard				
12/1048	4.2/5.2	2/1008	n	n

NOTES

I-8. Pale Beer: Traditional Pilsen & North German-Style Lagers

Pale colored beers with medium alcohol (3.8-4.5/4.8-5.7%), and rich assertive flavor. These are all-malt beers, originally brewed in what is now Czechoslovakia, and brewed according to the ancient purity law with four ingredients: water, malted barley and hops and yeast. Hop bouquet and taste are impressive. Original gravity 11-14/1044-56. Apparent extract 2.2-4.5/1009-18. Bitterness 25-45. Color 2-3.5/2.5-4.5SRM. Ingredients: very pale European 2-row Moravian barley malt from the traditional style of Pilsen and Bohemia, that is less fully modified (when compared with British or even U.S. malts of this type), and therefore requiring a long (up to 6-hours) "triple" decoction mash, in which portions of the mash are separated, brought to a boil, and then returned to the main mash to raise that temperature to proper levels for various enzyme actions which trigger conversion of starches and proteins necessary to the brewing process. Saazer are the traditional hops called for, and Pilsen water is soft at about 50ppm.

NORTH GERMAN LAGER
AND "PILS"

Compare **Becks** IN West Germany (below) with that made to be shipped to the U.S.(I-7), for an interesting comparison: higher original extract, bitterness, and no corn! The North German pale lager style differs from that of Czechoslovakia-Bohemia with slightly lower original extract (11-12/1044-48), paler color, dry taste and low beer gravity, somewhat lower alcohol, and a more pronounced hop nose (from hop oil added at bottling), coupled with slightly less actual i.b.u. from Hallertauer,

Spalt, Tettnanger or Bavarian Northern Brewer hops. Water hardness in the 200-400ppm range. Incidentally **Pinkus Ur-Pils** profiled below uses organic malt!

PROFILES

beer's gravity OP/OG	alcohol ww/vv	beer's AE/BG	hops ibu	color/SRM
Aass Pilsner (Nor)				
12.8/1051	4.2/5.3	2.7/1011	n	3.5
1896 **Anton Dreher Michelob** (Aust/Czk)				
11.3/1045	3.4/4.3	3.1/1013	35	n
1901 **Anton Dreher Pilsner** (Aust/Czk)				
10.8/1043	3.5/4.4	2.4/1010	40	n
Becks in West Germany				
12.3/1049	3.7/4.6	3.4/1013	28.5	n
1887 **Budweiss** (Czk)				
11.3/1045	3.5/4.4	2.8/1011	35	n
Pilsner Urquel (Czk)				
12.1/1048.4	3.45/4.3	3.7/1014	43	3/4.2 (10EBC)
Pinkus Ur-Pils (WG)				
11.1/1044	3.8/4.8	2.0/1008	n	3
1906 Bohemian, average 6 samples				
11.3/1045	3.4/4.3	3/1012	43	n

NOTES

I-9. Pale Beer: Dortmund-Style ("Export") Lagers

Very pale beers, a little stronger than Bohemian, but a little less hoppy. Dortmunder was one of the four great lager beer styles to evolve in Continental Europe during the nineteenth century. (The others were Pilsner, Munich, and Vienna, all named after their cities of origin.) Dortmund is noted for its very hard (over 1000ppm, 56 dH) water, and in this it is exceeded only by the famous Burton-on-Trent water.

Dortmund water, and its effect on the brewing cycle is probably the single most important factor in **Dortmund** beer after the very special Dortmund malting style, with increased enzyme power, very pale color. Today, in Germany, the actual Dortmund style beer is called "export." Original gravity 12.5-14.9/1050-61. Alcohol around 4.5/ 5.5%. Apparent extract (beer gravity) is usualy very low, because the beer is strongly attenuated (fully fermented, even forced fermented, to reduce dextrins in the beer) to around 2/1008, or less. Bitterness 24-37, between that of Pilsen and Munich beers.

Color very pale, like that of Pilsen beer, from 3-3.5/ 3.3-5SRM. Nugy (12) tells us that Dortmund beers should be less than 8 lovibond (SRM) in color (under 4.5, 1-10), and over 12.5/1050 in original extract. Ingredients, aside from the pale "Dortmund" malt, include some pale crystal malt and Hallertau, Spalt, Tettnang or Northern Brewer hops.

No current profiles, (need **DAB Original** profile), but:

1968 Dortmund beer
     12.9/1052   4.6/5.8   1.9/1007   24   2.5

NOTES

I-10. Pale Beer: Bavarian Helles (Pale) Lagers

Pale beer, similar to the Bohemian Pilsner style, but sweeter, heavier, yet similar in alcohol content, literally a pale (helles) version of the Munich beer (dunkel). The taste is more malty, and less hoppy with smooth, almost caramelly, undertones and, higher apparent extract. Original gravity 11.5-13.5/1046-55. Alcohol 3.6-4.4/4.5-5.5%. Fairly high apparent extract at about 3/1012. Bitterness 20-30. Color 2-3/2.6- 4.5SRM, slightly darker than regular Pils. This style originated in the early Twentieth century as Bavarian brewers finally reacted to the pale beers popular in the rest of Germany, and Europe. Pale two-row European barley malted at lower temperatures to produce a pale Munich malt with Bavarian Hallertauer or Northern Brewer hops, and medium hard water of about 200ppm hardness, are the usual ingredients. This beer style is popular around Germany, mostly in the south, a little heavier than the Pils type found in the north of that country.

PROFILES

beer's gravity OP/OG	alcohol ww/vv	beer's AE/BG	hops ibu	color/SRM
Altenmunster (WG)				
12.7/1051	4.6/5.6	1.7/1007	n	3/n
Ayinger Jahrhundert (WG-Bav)				
13/1052	4.1/5.2	3/1012	29.4	3.5
Kulmbacker Schweitzerhofbrau (WG)				
12.7/1051	3.9/4.9	2.8/1011	n	3.5/n
1977 Bavarian helles (5)				
11.8/1047	3.7/4.6	2.5/1010	2.7	2.5/3.7
1884 **Nurnberger Actien** (pale)				
14.8/1061	4.9/6.1	4.25/1017	n	n

NOTES

I-11. Pale and Amber Beer: Strong European-Style Bottom Fermented Beer.

Pale to very light amber in color, with variable hoppiness, but usually assertive; strong in alcohol, these may not be all- malt beers. Any strong lager (not including pale bocks) — "Starkbier" — 4.5-10/5.5-12.6% alcohol. Original gravity over 15/1060. Apparent extract usually over 2.5/1010. Bitterness 20-37. Color 2-3.5/2.5-4SRM. Pale 6-, or 2-row American or European malts, and perhaps some color malt, English, American or Euro hops, water hardness to 500ppm. This is an improvement on the American Malt Liquor. A classic example of this type is Danish **Carlsberg Elephant**, for which we have no profile, see similar Danish **Giraf** below.

PROFILES

beer's gravity OP/OG	alcohol ww/vv	beer's AE/BG	hops ibu	color/SRM
Giraf (Den)				
16.2/1066	5.8/7.3	2.4/1010	23.5	3/4.4

NOTES

I-12. Pale and Amber Beer: Top Fermented Blonde or Golden Ales (Traditional U.S. Cream Ale)

Americans once called this beer "cream ale" but that has come to be a bottled lager-ale (see I-4). Traditional cream ale was "present use ale," or sometimes "lively ale," a *real ale* draft beer of gravity at 13/1053, which was krausened with beer wort, rather than primed with sugar, and served in taverns directly from the wood. Today's cream ale is a far cry, but this style, which I have labeled blonde or golden ale fits that description fairly well, if we allow for the American style of service rather than real ale from the wood.

These are straw (blonde) to pale amber (golden) in color, medium alcohol, (3-4.5/3.8-5.7%), a "blonde" or "golden" version of the so-called "pale ales," with assertive to intense hop levels. This is a new and separate category only because it is becoming popular among new American brewers and doesn't really fit in the original or "pale ale" category. Original gravity 10-13.8/1040-61. Apparent extract 2.2-3.7/1009-15. Bitterness 20-40. Color 2.5-5/2.5-8SRM. These blonde ales differ from bottled American ales, or so-called "cream ales," in that they are not lagered, but brewed entirely as ales.

This beer incorporates ale-type ingredients, but is designed around malt that is paler than the typical British type ale-malt. These are (in the U.S., where the style is becoming popular) two-row Klages malted barley, plus caramel or Munich malt for minimum color, and American specialty hops from Oregon and sometimes Washington (Fuggles, Brewers Gold, Northern Brewer, Cascade or Willamettes, and sometimes even Perles).

PROFILES

beer's gravity OP/OG	alcohol ww/vv	beer's AE/BG	hops ibu	color/SRM
Ballard Bitter				
11.6/1046	3.8/4.8	2.5/1010	29	4
Boulder Sport (corn adjunct)				
11.5/1046	3.5/4.3	3.2/1013	22	n
BridgePort Golden Ale				
10.5/1042	3.75/4.7	1.5/1006	28	5
BridgePort Rose City Ale				
10.5/1042	3.3/4.1	2.6/1010	n	3
BridgePort Spring Draught				
11.5/1046	3.75/4.7	2.5/1010	70	4.5
Grant's India Pale Ale draft				
11.5/1046	3.8/4.8	2.4/1010	55	4.5
Portland Ale				
12/1048	4.0/5.0	2.4/1009	20	3.5
Winter Hook				
13.8/1056	4.4/5.5	3.2/1013	32	4
1901 U.S. Cream Ale				
13.6/1054	4.8/5.9	2.2/1009	40	n.

NOTES

● ● ●

II. AMBER BEER.
10 categories — 74 profiles.

Profile code: Specific beers are listed with their original gravity as degrees Plato (OP) and British gravity degrees (OG);alcohol content wt/vol; AE Plato/AG gravity; bitterness; and color 1-10/SRM.

For example:

Bass Pale Ale (E)
    11.8/1047   3.7/4.7   2.9/1011   19   5.5/9.8

Translation: original gravity 11-Plato/or gravity 1044: alcohol 3.7% by weight/or 4.7% by volume: apparent extract 2.1-Plato/or gravity 1008: bitterness 10.5 b.u.: color 2 (1-10) or 2-SRM. An "n" in one of the spaces indicates we do not have that particular information spec on the beer.

COLOR DEFINITIONS

Color 1-10 scale:		SRM*
0	water	0
1-1.5	light straw	1-2.5
1.5-2	pale straw	2.5-3.5
2-3.5	dark straw	3.5-5.5
3.5-4.5	light amber	5.5-10
4.5-5.5	pale amber	10-18
5.5-6.5	dark amber or copper	18-26
6.5-8.5	very dark amber "dark"	26-40
8.5-10	"black"	40 & up

*SRM = Standard Research Method degree, roughly equivalent to the old lovibond degree, and is used by the ASBC, (American Society of Brewing Chemists). In this system color is noted as degree SRM. The Europeans use a unit called "EBC (European Brewery Congress) degree." This is variable, but sometimes:
1 degree EBC = 2.65 degree SRM, less 1.2.
1 degree SRM = 0.375 EBC degree, plus 0.46.

II-1. Amber Beer: Amber and Vienna Lagers

This type of beer is amber or pale copper in color, and medium alcohol (3.8-4.5/4.8-5.6%). Style is almost identical to New American lagers (I-6), except for the slightly darker color. These are usually (but not necessarily) all-malt beers. The "amber" designation sometimes has little to do with actual color. If the brewery calls it "amber" or "Vienna" we agree. See also next category (II-2). Original gravity 11.5-13/1046-52. Apparent extract 2.2-4/1009-1016. Bitterness 18-35. Color between that of Munich or Bavarian beer and that of Pilsen or Bohemian beer, 4.5-6.5/10-20SRM. Nugy (12) tells us "Vienna" beer should be at least 12 lovibond (SRM) in color (about 5, 1-10 scale). Ingredients, 2-row barley malt, augmented with caramel color malt and dextrin malt for additional body, and possibly Munich or amber malt, but the preferred Vienna malts are difficult to obtain in this country, where the beer is becoming popular again. Hops — Central European types are preferred: Saaz, Zatec, or Styrian Goldings. The Vienna amber lager was first brewed by Anton Dreher in Vienna in the 1840's. Water hardness is around 200-400ppm.

PROFILES

beer's gravity OP/OG	alcohol ww/vv	beer's AE/BG	hops ibu	color/SRM
Ambier Genuine Vienna Style				
13/1052	4/5	3.4/1013	25	5
Dos Equis Amber (Mex)				
10.9/1044	3.7/4.6	2/1008	22	6
Island Pacific Key Lager (Can)				
10.2/1041	3.2/4	2.5/1010	14.5	5
1986 Newman's Albany Amber Beer				
10.5/1042	3.6/4.5	2.3/1009	18	4.5
Portland Lager				
12.5/1050	3.9/4.9	3.1/1012	26	5

NOTES

II-2. *Amber and Pale Beer: Vienna Style Seasonal Variations, Oktoberfest, Marzenbier, etc.*

This type of beer is amber or pale copper in color, and medium to strong alcohol (4-4.8/5-6%). Style originated in Vienna early in the nineteenth century, but is rarely made there now, although we have one sample, **Gosser** on our list. Some of these are made seasonally or, in some cases, labeled Oktoberfest, for example, but made the year around. If the brewery calls it "Oktoberfest" or "Festbier," we agree, even if it is a top fermented "alt," or German style ale, as are the **Widmer** beers listed among the profiles below. Original gravity 12.5- 14.9/1050-61. Bitterness 22-35. Color 4-6/8-14SRM. See Amber Lager (II-1) for ingredients.

PROFILES

beer's gravity OP/OG	alcohol ww/vv	beer's AE/BG	hops ibu	color/SRM
Aass Jul Ol (Nor)				
13.5/1055	4.5/5.7	2.7/1011	n	6.5
Ayinger Fest Maerzen (WG)				
12.9/1052	4.1/5.1	3.1/1013	22.5	5
Coors Winterfest				
16/1066	4.5/5.7	5.2/1020	17	4
Dixie Oktoberfest Draft				
11.5/1048	3.7/4.6	2.7/1011	22	4
Gosser (Austria)				
13.4/1054	4.3/5.4	2.4/1010	34	5

beer's gravity OP/OG	alcohol ww/vv	beer's AE/BG	hops ibu	color/SRM
Paulaner Oktoberfest (WG)				
13/1052	4.3/5.4	2.7/1011	n	5
Millstream Schildbrau				
13.5/1055	4.3/5.4	3.2/1013	n	5
1985 **Widmer Festbier Draft** (top ferm):				
14.8/1060	5.1/6.4	2.6/1010	25	5
1987 **Widmer Festbier Draft** (top ferm)				
14.1/1058	4.2/5.3	4/1016	30.6	6
1987 **Widmer Maerzen Draft** (top ferm)				
13/1052	3.9/4.9	3.6/1015	22	4.5

NOTES

II-3. Amber Beer: Biere de Garde, Biere de Paris

This is the French version of Vienna lager, strong beer: over 15-Plato/1060, and 5/6% alcohol. These beers are all-malt and quite delicious, strongly hopped, more so than the Vienna style. They are "laying-down" beers with cork finish, and improve with age in the bottle (up to about a year). The most popular sample **Brasseurs Biere de Paris** does not seem to fit the style profile, yet Jackson tells us it is a *biere de garde* — ah well. See amber lager (II-1) for an overview of ingredients.

PROFILE

beer's gravity OP/OG	alcohol ww/vv	beer's AE/BG	hops ibu	color/SRM
Brasseurs Biere de Paris (Fr)				
12.3/1049	4/5	2.8/1011	n	6.5

NOTES

II-4. Amber Beer: Pale Bocks and Other Strong Lagers

Pale amber in color, these beers are strong (alcohol 4.8-11/6-13.2%) with very assertive hoppiness, and all-malt in the Reinheitsgebot tradition. See also I-11. Original extract required by German law must be at least 16-Plato/1064 to be designated "bock." Bitterness 25-40. Color 3-5.5/5-9SRM, a little darker than most "pale" beers. These beers are brewed from mostly pale 2-row Bohemian style barley malt augmented variously by dark Munich and caramel malts, and in some cases pale dextrin malt will also be used (for additional body). The brewer's regular hops will be used in most cases, but the European hops, such as Hallertauer or Northern Brewer will be preferred. The **Samichlaus Hell** (below) is fermented with a "special" yeast, which may be top or bottom yeast — we've not found out for sure.

PROFILES

beer's gravity OP/OG	alcohol ww/vv	beer's AE/BG	hops ibu	color/SRM
Ayinger Maibock (WG)				
17.2/1071	5.5/6.9	4.1/1016	26.5	3
1884 **Dortmund Victoria**				
16/1064	4.5/5.7	4.8/1019	40	n
Island Bock (Can)				
17.6/1072	5.2/6.5	5.5/1022	25	5.5
Kulmbacker Schwiezerhofbrau Bock (WG)				
16.1/1066	5.7/7.1	2.4/1010	n	4
1907 **Pschorr Marzenbier** (Ger-Bav)				
16.4/1067	4.9/6.2	4.3/1017	30	n
1987 **Samichlaus Bier** — pale				
27.6/1116	11.2/14.1	n	5	
				bright copper
1988 **Widmer Bock**				
15.9/1065	5.5/6.9	3/1012	31	4.5

NOTES

II-5. Amber or Dark Beer: California Common Beer (Steam Beer)

Warm temperature ferments using bottom yeast produce beers with an ale character. The style was invented in California, where it was called "steam beer." These beers may have any taste profile or color, but most are amber, with medium to strong alcohol, noticeable to intense hop bouquet, and rather assertive taste. The steam beer style was made all over the west coast, including Alaska and Idaho, and as far east as Wisconsin. Steam beers were amber or dark. They presented a darker version of what was then called *Cream Ale*, a paler, top fermented beer with much the same characteristics.

The original "steam beers" and "cream ales" were top and bottom fermented versions of what we now call *real ale*, that is they were fermented warm, not too well aged, and served as "present use" beers. The old wooden beer kegs were krausened with fresh beer wort, in the German fashion, rather than primed with sugar as the English do. Modern cream ales are bottled American lagered ales, and modern steam beer is a trademark of the Anchor Brewing Company. See also I-12. Ingredients: 2- or 6-row American barley malt, plus up to 10% caramel malt, and (brewer's preference) maybe some darker malts for extra color. Washington Northern Brewer hops preferred.

California common beer (steam beer) will not have been lagered cold, but may have been stored at cellar temperatures (55°F/12.8°C). Original gravity 11-14/1044-56 or so. Alcohol 3.6-4.5/4.6-5.6%. Bitterness 20-45. Color 3.5. Wahl (15) **California Steam Beer** recipe: 11-12.5/1044-50 including 33% adjuncts and sugars, 35 bitterness, and color as amber as Munich beer, i.e. 5-6 on our scale (10-20SRM). **Kentucky Common Beer** recipe 10-12.5/1040-50, 27 bitterness and 2% *lactobaccilum* in the yeast. This was a dark beer, 6-8.5. **Pennsylvania Swankey,** flavored with anise seed or similar, boiled 30-min in the wort: 7/1028 and 22 bitterness.

PROFILES

beer's gravity OP/OG	alcohol ww/vv	beer's AE/BG	hops ibu	color/SRM
Anchor brand **San Francisco Steam Beer**				
12.5/1050	3.7/4.6	3.4/1013	40	5
1972 **San Francisco Steam Beer**				
12.5/1050	3.7/4.6	3.6/1014	45	5
1948 **SF Steam Beer** (w/ corn)				
11.5/1046	3.⅓.9	4/1016	40	n
1907 Kentucky Common Beer (2 samples)				
12.2/1049	3.1/3.8	4.7/1019	27	n

NOTES

II-6. *Amber Beer: British Standard Ale — Bitters and Best Bitters.*

These top fermented ales are very similar to pale ales (see next), and sometimes they are identical. In England the one and the other are often the same, but pale ales are more often bottled beers, while bitters are mostly draught beers. Here we differentiate British ordinary ales as those pale ales of lower original gravity, 7.5-11.5/1030-1046, which is more in keeping with reality, even in England. Their taste is rather mild to assertive, with medium or even low alcohol content, 3.8/4.8% or less (usually). Bitterness in the 10-30 range. Color 4-6/8- 12SRM. Ingredients similar to those called for in pale ale (next II-7).

"Real Ales" are, by definition, fermented (conditioned, or naturally carbonated) in the manner of classical Champagne; that is, in the container from which they are dispensed. When found in the bottle they are called bottle conditioned. Bottled "real ales" will have a yeast sediment. Such beers should be decanted when served. On draught in England, as noted earlier, these beers are usually called "bitter," or "best bitter."

Hough *et al* (6) quotes (1981) original extract 7.5-11.3/ 1030-1045; alcohol 2.2-3.5/2.8-4.4%; bitterness 28-38; and color 15-60 EBC (6.1-23SRM, about 4-8 on our 1-10 color scale). This for "British fined beer" (i.e. "real ale"), while keg beer (CO_2 injected) with similar gravity and alcohol, and rated at 17-35 bitterness, and color 6-90EBC (2.7-34SRM, about 2-8.5). The same source gives us 1960 draught bitter ("real ale") at original extract 7.7-11.3/1031-1045; 2.3-3.7/3-4.6% alcohol; and 20-40 bitterness. "Light bottled ale" at 7.7-9.7/1031-1039; 2.3- 3.2/2.9-4% alcohol with

16-38 bitterness. These parameters are mostly from various draught beers, and they reflect the British drinker's requirements. The British consume most of their beer in public houses ("pubs"), and the alcohol content is necessarily lower than Americans demand, because of this fact. It is very unwise to sit in a bar and drink 4% beer over a long period of time, hence the British proclivity towards lower alcohol levels. Such beer is in no way as tasteless as American "lite" beers, if it were there would be much lower consumption in that country, because the American low alcohol style beer is entirely too tasteless to be consumed in quantity.

Just for the record, Richardson's *Science and Brewing*, 6th Ed., ca 1805 (10) quotes small beer at original gravity 6.7/1026, apparent extract 1.9/1007, alcohol 2/2.5%, probably very dark, and more than likely soured quickly. Richardson invented the hydrometer, and was the first to use a thermometer in malting and mashing.

PROFILES

beer's gravity OP/OG	alcohol ww/vv	beer's AE/BG	hops ibu	color/SRM
Belhaven Scottish Ale (E / 80 shilling ale)				
10.3/1041	3.3/4.1	2.3/1009	n	6.5
1985 **Boulder Pale Ale**				
11.5/1046	3.8/4.8	2.4/1009	29	6
BridgePort Harvest Bitter				
11.5/1046	3.85/4.8	2.3/1009	30	5.5
BridgePort Ski Draught				
10/1040	2.9/3.7	3/1012	23	n
Hale's Bitter Draught				
11.2/1045	3.8/4.8	2.1/1008	44	6.5

beer's gravity OP/OG	alcohol ww/vv	beer's AE/BG	hops ibu	color/SRM
Hale's Pale American Ale				
9/1036	2.9/3.6	2/1008	36	6
Pacific Crest Ale				
11/1044	3.5/4.4	2.6/1010	27	6.5
Pyramid Pale Ale				
11/1044	3.5/4.4	2.6/1010	40	6.5
Young's RamRod (E)				
11.5/1046	3.8/4.8	2.4/1010	38	6

NOTES

II-7. Amber Beers: Pale Ales

Pale ales are usually not very pale. They were called pale only because they were lighter in color to the then popular porters, and are actually amber to dark 4-7/8-12SRM in color, with alcohol under 5/6.2%. Taste ranges from assertive to downright strong, hops mild to very intense, hop bouquet noticeable to intense (bitterness 20-50). There is a very wide range in these beers. Gravity from 11.6/1046 to 14.9/1061. These are a British style of beer, and should all be top fermented. Pale ales are a generic term embracing a wide range of brews. These usually include the "bitter" and "best bitter," which we have moved into a separate class (above, II-6). "Pale ales" are heavier, more often bottled, and sometimes they may be found bottle conditioned as well. This product is dry, hoppy and well fermented, with a lower apparent extract. Wahl (15) offers a 1900 London pale ale 14/1057 and 76 bitterness. See also blonde or golden ales (paler pale ales and bitters, I-12).

Ingredients include the British style (darker) 2-row pale (ale) malts, which are well modified (compared to Continental lager malts, and even when compared to U.S. malts) in the malting process to make them more easily converted in the simple single temperature or one-step infusion mashing method used by British brewers. Additional malts are used in pale and bitter ales, and these might include crystal malt (40, 60, 80, or higher lovibond), along with amber, and even brown or chocolate malt, according to the brewer's desire. British brewers often use sugar, and are not above adding grain adjuncts to their beer. British type Golding, Bullion or Fuggle hops are mandated, and beers are frequently dry hopped, that is, hops are added in storage, giving the beer a wonderful hop bouquet when opened or tapped in the barrel. British brewers prefer their hops with some seed content. Water hardness varies from 250 to 1700ppm. Hough *et al* (6) quotes 1960 "best pale" at original extract 10.1-12.6/1040-50; alcohol 3.4-5.2/4.3-6.6%; and 19-55 bitterness. See further notes in previous category (II-6) concerning British "draught beers" and "real ales."

Richardson (10) gives us an 1805 table beer at 13.3/1054 gravity and apparent extract at 5.3/1021 (sweet — if not sour!), but alcohol a modest 3.3/4.2%. Quickly brewed, quickly consumed.

American-type bottom fermented ales are found in other categories: i.e. American ales, strong ales, American common beer (steam beer), or strong lagers.

We present a number of pale ale profiles because there is such a great variety in this beer style, here and in England.

PROFILES

beer's gravity OP/OG	alcohol ww/vv	beer's AE/BG	hops ibu	color/SRM
Anchor Liberty Ale				
14.8/1061	4.8/6	3.3/1013	45	5.5
1975 **Anchor Liberty Ale**				
14.8/1061	4.8/6	3.3/1013	54	5.5
Bass Pale Ale (E)				
11.8/1047	3.7/4.7	2.9/1011	19	5.5/9.8
Boulder Pale Ale				
12.5/1050	4.3/5.3	2.3/1009	29	6
BridgePort Ale				
12/1048	3.5/4.4	3.6/1014	27	6.5
Grant's Scottish Ale				
13.4/1054	4.5/5.6	2.7/1011	45	5.5
Hopland Red Tail Ale				
13.5/1055	4.4/5.5	2.9/1012	45	5

PROFILES

beer's gravity OP/OG	alcohol ww/vv	beer's AE/BG	hops ibu	color/SRM
1986 Newman's Tricentennial Pale Ale				
12.2/1049	4/5	2.5/1010	26	5
Oregon Trail Ale				
12/1048	3.6/4.5	3.4/1014	22	6
Red Hook Ale				
12.8/1051	4.5/5.7	2/1008	18	6.5
Royal Oak Pale Ale (E)				
12.2/1049	3.7/4.7	3.4/1013	n	6.5
Samuel Smith Pale Ale (E)				
12/1048	3.7/4.6	3.2/1013	25.5	6
Sierra Nevada Pale Ale				
13.9/1057	4.4/5.5	2.3/1009	32	6
Whitbread Pale Ale (E)				
13.5/1055	4.6/5.8	2.7/1011	25.5	5
1906 American Pale Ale				
13/1053	4/5	3.6/1014	60	n

NOTES

II-8. Pale and Amber Beer: Kolsch & Other German Ales or Altbiers (blonde to pale & amber)

Most German beers in the alt-bier category (Alt-bier = old beer, i.e., beer made in the old style) are top/warm fermented. **Kolsch** is blonde altbier from Koln (Cologne), very pale in color, with a noticeabale, but not intense, taste profile. **Kolsch** is an appellation, whose parameters are carefully defined by German law (Narziss): original gravity 11.2-11.8/1045-47; color 7.5-14EBC (2.5-4/3.3-5.7SRM); 16-34 bitterness; water hardness 26DH (450ppm); primary ferment at 18-22°C (64-72°F); secondary ferment 14-18°C (57-64°F); lager 14-40 days, and the product must be filtered; but a German court held this was not an absolute requirement, if the product was labeled as unfiltered. **Kolschbier** has Vienna malt, and up to 20% wheat malt plus the usual Pilsen type along with darker Bavarian and caramel malts in its makeup. Hops would include Hallertauer, Perle, or Spalt. See II-10 (Belgian Trappist) for the only other beer appellation in this list.

The alt-bier styles range, in color, from blonde to very deep amber, but they are listed with dark beers, (III-6). Alt-bier is the German version of pale ale, although today these beers are usually finished out with cold aging, as is done in lager production, following a warm ferment with top fermenting yeast. Bottle conditioned alts (hefe-), when found, are usually conditioned with lager yeast rather than ale yeast.

Rheinland Bitter Beer is a top fermented golden beer, strongly hopped, and filtered similar to lager beer.

Maisel Dampf is a modern top fermented beer,

developed (according to Jackson) in the late 1970's, and is, therefore, not considered an "alt-bier." We use the term here as equal to top fermented ale style beer, rather than in its true and more limited German meaning.

PROFILES

beer's gravity OP/OG	alcohol ww/vv	beer's AE/BG	hops ibu	color/SRM
Gaffel Kolsch (in WG)				
11.6/1046	3.9/5	1.8/1007	31	4/4.9
Maisel Dampfbier (WG)				
12.2/1059	4/5	2.6/1010	n	5
Stecken Kolsch (in WG)				
11.2/1045	3.8/4.8	2.2/1009	21	2.5/3.4
Sunner Kolsch (in WG)				
11.5/1046	4/5	1.9/1008	21.5	4/5.5

NOTES

II-9. Amber and Dark Beer: Strong Ale, Burton Ale, Scottish Ale, Old Ale, and Old India Pale Ale

Strong ales are usually darker in color than other pale ales and often assertively hopped. They are usually top or warm fermented, and often are fully attenuated or well fermented to reduce apparent extract or beer gravity, and a dry palate. The range in strength from 4.8-6/6-7.6%. They make fine "nitecap" beers. Original extract 15-17.5/1060-70. These are often highly hopped beers with bitterness in the 20-60 range. Color 3.5-7/8-13SRM (but up to 45 in Old ales). Hough *et al* (6) quotes 1960 strong ales (including barleywines) at original extract 16.1-19/1066-78; alcohol 4.9-6.7/6.1-8.4 and 25-43 bitterness with color up to 90EBC (34SRM, about 8.5 on our 1-10 scale).

Richardson gives us an 1805 "ale" (his strong ale tops 25/1100) at 15.4/1063, apparent at 5.4/1021, and alcohol 4.2/5.2.

Wahl (15) offers turn of the century American stock ale at 17/1070 with 25% sugar and 108 bu, and Burton Export Ale at 17.5/1072 at 152 bitterness!

SCOTTISH ALE

Scottish Ale is merely strong ale similar to the above, but made with Scotch malts, which are different from those used in English ales, and indeed in the early days, they probably imparted a smokey flavor to the beer, from having been dried with peat moss kilning. Modern Scottish or Scotch ales have more sweet maltiness, although little of the smokey character that endeared them to folks in their beginnings. They are almost thick from aromatic pale 2-row British type malts, and high gravity worts (up to 20/1082). Scottish ales often incorporate darker malts, notably amber and brown, plus some chocolate malt, and perhaps treacle or brown sugar in the kettle. They are less hoppy than their English counterparts. They are popular now, and are found frequently in Belgium, and even France. Jackson (7a) tells us Scottish ale is "less hoppy, more malty, fuller bodied [and] with more residual sweetness." It should be noted that other beers called "Scottish ales" are more in the mild/brown ale range (III-5), or even (at least by our notation) as bitter or "British standard" ales (II-7), e.g. **Belhaven** in that category.

INDIA PALE ALE

India Pale Ale is a strong ale which was made in England, shipped to India (by sail), in a rather long voyage. In the process the beer went (in wooden barrels) from cold England, to equatorial heat, and then to cold again rounding the Cape of Good Hope (S. Africa) and then up to India, crossing the equator once more. The beer was, of course, subject to wave action and the constant movement of a long sea voyage, over a several month period. When the beer finally arrived at its destination in India, it was found to have an especially fine taste. In this manner, the fame of Old India Pale Ale spread, but it originated as an ale which had been mistreated. These days it is usually presented as very pale in color (4-5.5/6-18SRM), from pale malts only, or pale with a little crystal malt. Today this is a distinctly pale beer in most versions, even to the point of being in the color range of our blonde or golden ale category (I-12), but it is basically a strong ale, although some low gravity examples may be found, i.e., **Grant's India Pale Ale** from Yakima, WA.

Nugy (12) offers 1948 advice to original gravity

over 15/1062, and color under 8 lovibond (SRM), 4.5, in the 1-10 scale, a distinctly pale or blonde beer.

See next category (II-10) and also III-9, (barleywines).

PROFILES

beer's gravity OP/OG	alcohol ww/vv	beer's AE/BG	hops ibu	color/SRM
1979 Ballantines Old India Pale Ale:				
18.5/1076	6.1/7.7	3.9/1015	45	5.5
1896 Bass Pale Ale (E)				
15/1062	5.6/7	1.8/1007	87	n
1987 BridgePort Winterbrew Strong Ale				
15/1062	4.6/5.8	4/1016	40	n
Sierra Nevada Celebration Ale				
16/1066	5.1/6.4	3.8/1015	45	6
Hales Wee Heavy				
16.6/1068	5.7/7.1	3.3/1013	38	5
1976 Rainier Ale (bottom fermented)				
15/1061	5.7/7.1	1.3/1005	19	5.5
Young's Special London Ale (E)				
15.1/1062	5/6.2	3.5/1014	56	6
1907 U.S. Old India Pale Ale, Hudson NY, with 23% sugar				
16.5/1068	5.4/6.8	3.2/1012	60	n
1907 U.S. Stock Ale				
16.3/1067	5.3/6.7	3.3/1013	50	n

NOTES

II-10. Amber Beer: Strong Belgian Ales — amber or pale

These are similar to the last category, but Belgian beers tend to enjoy a wider range of flavors contributed by various yeast strains, which may also have accompanying bacteria, in the manner of all top fermented beer in the "old" days. Some are fermented with as many as three different yeast strains, one in primary ferment, another in secondary ferment, and a third in the bottle, real ale style. Alcohol over 5/6.3%. See strong ales, especially Scottish Ales for ingredient suggestions. Belgian ales often incorporate "candy" sugar or glucose chips (called dextrose in the U.S.). Belgian brewers sometimes add aromatics, such as coriander, cumin and ginger following 17th Century Scottish practice.

SAISON

Saison is a Belgian summer seasonal beer of Liege, and often only about 50% attenuated (fermented). They are sharply refreshing, and usually have the distinctive and easily recognized Belgian character.

Strong Belgian beers are listed in the "Trappist" category (II-11), and where pertinent — over 7.2 Belg or 18/1072 — in the "barleywine" category (III-9) as "triples."

PROFILES

beer's gravity OP/OG	alcohol ww/vv	beer's AE/BG	hops ibu	color/SRM
OE Belgian degree listed under OG				
Augustijn (B)				
16.3/1067 6.7 Belg	5.9/7.5	2.5/1010	n	5.5
Duvel (B)				
14.9/1061 6.1 Belg	5/6.4	2.8/1011	n	3.5

NOTES

II-11. Amber, Pale & Dark Beer:
Belgian Trappist Ales

This is not a single style of beer, but "Trappiste" is a protected appellation in Belgium, and the standards are guaranteed by the governing body. Each is different and distinctive in the manner of Belgian ales, and each is a unique product in its own right.

See categories II-9, especially Scottish ales, II-10 (Belgian strong ales) and III-9 (Barleywine ales) for some similar parameters. See II-8 Kolschbier, for the only other beer "Appelation" in these files.

PROFILES

beer's gravity OP/OG	alcohol ww/vv	beer's AE/BG	hops ibu	color/SRM
OE Belgian degree listed below OG.				
Chimay (red)				
15.4/1063	5.5/7	2.3/1009	n	6.5
6.3 Belg				
Chimay Grand Reserve (blue)				
19/1078	7.1/8.9	2.6/1010	n	6
7.8 Belg				
Orval				
13.7/1056	4.8/6	2.5/1010	24	5
5.6 Belg				
St.Sixtus				
18.3/1075	7.8/9.8	2.4/1010	11.2	9
7.5 Belg				

NOTES

● ● ●

III. DARK BEERS
9 categories — 73 profiles.

Profile code: Specific beers are listed with their original gravity as degrees Plato (OP) and British gravity degrees (OG);alcohol content wt/vol; AE Plato/AG gravity; bitterness; and color 1-10/SRM.

For example:
Henry Weinhard Special Reserve Dark
    12/1048   3.7/4.6   3/1012   16   7

Translation: original extract 12 Plato/or gravity 1048: alcohol 3.7% by weight/or 4.6% by volume: apparent extract 2.5 Plato/or gravity 1010: bitterness 45 b.u.: color 7 (1-10 scale). No SRM is noted, as that spec is unknown. An "n" in any other space indicates we also do not have that particular information spec on the beer.

COLOR DEFINITIONS

Color 1-10 scale:		SRM*
0	water	0
1-1.5	light straw	1-2.5
1.5-2	pale straw	2.5-3.5
2-3.5	dark straw	3.5-5.5
3.5-4.5	light amber	5.5-10
4.5-5.5	pale amber	10-18
5.5-6.5	dark amber or copper	18-26
6.5-8.5	very dark amber "dark"	26-40
8.5-10	"black"	40 & up

*SRM = Standard Research Method degree, roughly equivalent to the old lovibond degree, and is used by the ASBC, (American Society of Brewing Chemists). In this system color is noted as degree SRM. The Europeans use a unit called "EBC (European Brewery Congress) degree." This is variable, but sometimes:
1 degree EBC = 2.65 degree SRM, less 1.2.
1 degree SRM = 0.375 EBC degree, plus 0.46.

III-1. Dark Beers: American Dark Lager

Most American dark lagers are similar to their pale counterparts (except for color). They are usually not as dark as the German original. Often they are simply dark amber in color. As in their pale versions, there is usually a lower taste profile, minimal hopping, and a lack of aroma or bouquet. The aroma is grainy or corn-y, as is that of the North American standard. Some of these differ from their "light" counterpart, only in being darkened with brewer's caramel syrup, rather than the dark malts expected of this category. Ingredients are identical to American Standard (I-2), except for the inclusion of caramel, Munich or black malt for color. Original extract 10-12/1040-48. Alcohol 3.2-4/4-5%. Apparent extract 1.2-3.7/1005-15. Bitterness 9-15. Color (many are actually amber in color, but we Americans perceive this style as "dark" no matter the color), 4-6/5-14SRM.

PROFILES

beer's gravity OP/OG	alcohol ww/vv	beer's AE/BG	hops ibu	color/SRM
Gartenbrau Dark				
13/1052	4/5	3.4/1014	n	7/n
Henry Weinhard Special Reserve Dark				
11.4/1046	3.7/4.6	2.6/1010	15	7/n
Noche Buena (Mex)				
10.8/1043	3.6/4.6	2.2/1009	27	7/n
Ulmer Braun				
12.1/1049	4.3/5.4	1.9/1007	n	6/n
1908 American all-malt, 9 samples				
14.3/1059	4.3/5.4	3.8/1015	28	n

NOTES

III-2. Dark Beers: American Style Bock Beer

These are almost identical with American dark beers, except that they may be a bit more pale in color (3.5-6/4.5-12SRM. They, too, are often brewed as pale beer, but with caramel syrup added. Only a few are "proper" American bock beers. These have dark malts, such as Munich and/or caramel (40L), plus dextrin malt and black malt, with American hops, Clusters and Cascades, for example, and medium alcohol, 3.8-4/4.8-5%. As a class they are much less assertive, with lower original gravities, and less alcohol than their much stronger European counterparts. All are seasonally issued, usually around mid-February each year. The American bock style originated in Wisconsin as a lower gravity "bock" for the American market.

Nugy (12) sets American bock beer (1948) to original extract of at least 13/1053 and color 15 Lovibond (SRM) or 7 on our 1-10 scale. He gives a four recipes at 12, 13, 14, & 15 Plato/1048, 53, 57, & 1062, with 14-25% added caramel malt, and about 35% adjunct, and 18-25 bitterness. At best a far cry from the German standard of 16/1066 gravity and all-malt structure (see III-4).

No current profile, but:

beer's gravity OP/OG	alcohol ww/vv	beer's AE/BG	hops ibu	color/SRM
1985 Lucky Bock				
11.6/1046	3.6/4.5	3/1012	16	6.5/n
1908 Milwaukee bocks avg				
13/1052	3.4/4.3	4.7/1019	n	n

III-3. Dark Beers: Munich or Bavarian Style Lagers.

These lager beers are not especially dark, but rather more dark-amber to brown in color, 5-7.5/14-20SRM, with medium alcohol, 3.8-4.8/4.8-6.3%. The taste is more malty, and less hoppy, with smooth, almost caramelly, undertones. Original gravity 12.5-14.5P/1050-58, apparent extract about 3/1012 and bitterness around 20-30. Ingredients are pale and dark Munich malts, plus black and caramel malts and Hallertauer hops, hardness around 250ppm. This modern Munich style beer was brewed in the early nineteenth century by Gustav Sedylmeyer at his Spatenbrau Munich brewery.

ERLANGER

The **Erlanger** style of beer originated in Erlangen in the Nurnberg-Franconia area of northern Bavaria. The **Erlangers** are heavier in gravity than the usual Munich beers, more in the 13-13.5/1053-55 extract range, and perhaps just a little darker.

KULMBACHER

Kulmbacher beer is heavier again than that of Erlangen, and it was the Kulmbach style which inspired the Munich brewers to improve their own style. Gravities in the 14-15/1057-1062 range, make this beer a richly enjoyable type for those long winter evenings.

SCHWARZBIER

In other parts of Germany these dark lagers will simply be called **Schwarzbier**, black beer. Kunze

(7a) suggests 12/1048 original gravity, Pilsen type hopping (25-45 i.b.u.) and color malts.

PROFILES

beer's gravity OP/OG	alcohol ww/vv	beer's AE/BG	hops ibu	color/SRM
Ayinger Alt-Bayrisches Dunkel (WG)				
13/1052	3.9/4.8	3.8/1015	23.5	7
1879 **Einbecker** (Ger)				
13.7/1056	4.0/5.0	4/1016	40	n
1875 **Erlanger** (Ger)				
13.1/1053	4.1/5.1	3.4/1014	38	n
1887 **Kulmbacker** (Ger)				
15.3/1063	4.5/5.6	4.5/1018	35	n
1867 **Lowenbrau** (in Germany)				
13.7/1056	3.6/4.5	4.8/1019	28	n
Monkshof Kloster Schwarz (WG)				
12.5/1050	2/5/1010	n	7	
1867 **Spatenbrau** (Ger)				
13.1/1053	3.2/4.1	4.5/1018	30	n
1901 **Wurzburger** (Ger)				
15/1062	4.1/5.1	5.4/1021	35	n
1901 Munich — 6 samples average				
14.1/1057	3.9/4.9	4.5/1017	40	n

NOTES

III-4. Dark Beer: European Bocks, Doppelbocks, and Strong Darks (Usually Bottom Fermented).

These lagers are usually darker than the Munich style beers, but are still not as dark as stout, for example. They are strong, by definition. In addition to the bocks and doppelbocks, we note strong lagers (over 15/1062 or so). Bocks are brewed classically, and by German law, at over 16/1066, with 4.8/6.6% alcohol. These beers are heavier versions of the Bavarian style described previously. Wahl (15) offers a **Kulmbacher** bock beer at 18-19/1074-78 gravity, similar to Bavarian Munich, but much stronger, and including dark Munich, dark caramel, dextrin and black malts, resulting in darker color and a sweeter palate. Water hardness at about 250ppm, bitterness 20-35.

EINBECKER

The "bock" beer style itself originated in the Bavarian city of Einbeck. It was brewed traditionally at the beginning of the fall brewing season (Sept 29), and sold the first day of spring. Munich soon adopted the beer and the style as well. You could almost say **Einbecker** was the beer that made Munich famous.

DOPPELBOCKS

Doppelbocks are required to be brewed at 18/1074, with 6/7.5% alcohol. There is a level of sweetness present in most, as evidenced by the hefty apparent extract of some at 4-6/1016- 24. Malt flavors predominate, and hop levels are relatively unassertive, although noticeable. The high alcohol content lends a "barleywine" flavor to some, and indeed doppelbocks do fit the barleywine profiles, except they are bottom fermented. Most German doppelbocks have names ending with an *-ator* suffix, e.g. Salv*ator*, which is the original of type. Bitterness 25-40 or so. Color about 7-8.5/18-35SRM. **Doppelbocks** have pale Munich, plus dark Munich, caramel, dextrin and black malts in their makeup, plus good old Hallertauer hops.

EISBOCK

These are extra-strong *doppelbocks* created by freezing the beer ("ice-bock"), and removing some of the water in the form of ice. This has the result of concentrating the beer, making it much stronger, and sweeter-tasting on the palate. See **EKU 28** profiles listed below.

PROFILES

beer's gravity OP/OG	alcohol ww/vv	beer's AE/BG	hops ibu	color/SRM
1878 **Bremer Doppelt** (Ger)				
23.3/1096 9.2/11.6		1/1004	30	n
Celebrator (WG)				
18.2/1075 5.5/6.9		5/1020	n	8.5
1878 **Doppelspaten**				
25.3/1106 7/8.8		8.5/1034	30	n
1878 **Einbecker Bock**				
18.1/1074 5.4/6.8		5.2/1021	30	n
1983 **EKU 28** (WG)				
28.8/1121 9.4/11.8		9.2/1037	29.5	6
1987 **EKU 28** (WG)				
27.5/1116 9.3/11.6		5.3/1021	26	6
Island Bock (Can)				
18/1074 5.2/6.5		5.5/1022	25	5.5
1880 **Kulmbacher Actien** (Ger)				
20.2/1083 5.3/6.6		7/1028	35	n
1888 **Kulmbacher** (Ger)				
17.6/1072 4.2/5.2		7.7/1031	35	n
Kulmbacker Schwiezerhofbrau Bock (WG)				
16.1/1066 5.7/7.1		2.4/1010	n	4

PROFILES

beer's gravity OP/OG	alcohol ww/vv	beer's AE/BG	hops ibu	color/SRM

Paulaner Salvator (WG)

| 18.3/1075 | 6.2/7.7 | 3.3/1013 | 26.5 | 7 |

1887 **Paulaner Salvator** (Ger)

| 18.8/1077 | 4.6/5.8 | 7.7/1031 | 28 | 7 |

NOTES

III-5. Dark Beer: Mild Ales, Brown Ales and Dark Ales (Top Fermented)

These top fermented ales range from amber to rich brown in color, taste rather mild to assertive, and medium or low alcohol, 2.6/3.3% or so. In some ways they are a little like porter, yet paler, sweeter, mellower, not as dry, and usually lower in alcohol. We have classified what, in England, are called "strong brown ales" as either strong ales or pale ales, depending on original gravity. Original extract 8-11/1032-44. Bitterness 10-30 from the English type hops, Golding, Bullion, Fuggle, etc. Color usually over 4.5/10-26. These beers have the darker color and sweeter palate from pale malts plus brown and chocolate malts. Water hardness in the 250ppm range.

Jackson (7a) distinguishes between southern English brown ales **Newcastle Brown** and **Vaux Double Maxim** (low gravity – 11.2/1045 – sweet, and very dark) and northern English brown ales as dryer from higher gravity worts and paler copper color.

Hough, *et al* (6) gives "draught mild" at 7.7-9.1/1031-37; alcohol 2-2.9/2.5-3.6; with 14-37 bitterness, and "brown ale" (usually bottled) 7.5-10.2/1030-41; alcohol 2-2.9/2.5-3.6; bitterness 16-28, and color up to EBC90/34SRM (about 8, 1-10).

Mild ale wasn't always so, from Wahl (15), we find London four ale (mild): 13.5/1055, and 60 bitterness, which would be quite acceptable as pale ale, and in England might even be considered "strong." How far the mighty have fallen!

I've included a European brown beer in this category, although it may be bottom fermented; **Gosser Stiftsbrau** is reddish colored and rather sweet for my taste. "Stiftsbrau" means abbey beer, this one was originally from the Benedictines.

PROFILES

beer's gravity OP/OG	alcohol ww/vv	beer's AE/BG	hops ibu	color/SRM
Gosser Stiftsbrau (Austria)				
13/1053	2.9/3.6	6/1024	n	8
Grant's Celtic Ale (bottled)				
8/1034	2.5/3.1	2/1008	38	
Hillsdale Nut Brown Ale				
13.1/1053	4.1/5.1	3.3/1013	31	7
Samuel Smith Nut Brown Ale (E)				
12.3/1049	4.4/5.4	1.7/1007	n	7
need profile **Newcastle Brown**				

NOTES

III-6. Dark and Amber Beer: Alt-Bier.

These top fermented beers range in color from deep amber to rich brown, with taste mild to assertive, and hop levels noticeable to assertive. Some dark alts are almost brown in color from the Munich and Vienna (Gerstenmalz) or amber malt in their makeup. Alt simply means "old," that is, beer fermented in the old style, or top fermented. These beers are fermented warm in the fashion of ales, and then aged cold as lager beers (14-40 days). Altbier may, and frequently does, have a portion of wheat in its makeup. This is usually in the neighborhood of 10-15% (Dusseldorf), but **Pinkus Alt** (Munster) has about 40% wheat malt. Typical ingredient formulas include 2-row Bohemian type malt, light and dark Munich and/or caramel malt, dextrin malt and perhaps a touch of black malt. Original extract 11-12/1044-48. Alcohol 3.5-4/4.5-5%. Apparent extract around 2.7/1011. Bitterness 28-40. Color 5.5-6.5/10-16SRM.

PROFILES

beer's gravity OP/OG	alcohol ww/vv	beer's AE/BG	hops ibu	color/SRM
Pinkus Alt (WG)				
11.3/1045	3.8/4.8	2.7/1011	n	5
Rheinisch Alt (in WG)				
11.8/1047	3.7/4.6	2.9/1011	26.5	n
Weihenstephen Alt (in WG)				
12/1040	3.9/4.9	2.8/1011	27	6/11
Widmer Alt				
11.5/1047	3.75/4.7	2.5/1010	45	7
1883 **Von Appels Alt** (Munster — in WG)				
12.3/1049	4.4/5.6	1.3/1005	n	n

NOTES

III-7. Black Beer: Porters

This style originated in mid-eighteenth century England as porter. As the beer style came to be brewed stronger, the name stout porter came into use indicating stronger porter. These have become known as stouts. Today, porters are usually medium strong beers with rich dry maltiness and intense hoppy flavors. The distinction between porter and stout is somewhat ephemeral, particularly in England, and Jackson is no less confusing on the point. For our purposes we can say that porters are dry, and if not they might better be classed as brown ale or as English (sweet) stout. Original gravity 12-14/1048-56 or so. Alcohol content 4/5-4.6/5.6%. Apparent extract around 2.8/1011. Bitterness over 25. Color above 24-36/8. If a beer is called "porter" we agree, but the fact remains that some "porters" (i.e. **Anchor Porter**) would be better judged as a stout (next). What did Wahl (15) have to say about porter? American porter 13/1052, 25% sugar, 54 bitterness, and English porter 14/1056, also 25% sugar, 30 bitterness. How about that?

Richardson (8A) describes 1805 porter at 15.8/1065 gravity, apparent at 3.8/1015, with alcohol 5/6.3% made with some molasses added in the kettle (20%?).

Porter is also brewed with bottom yeast in this country, plus such diverse places as Denmark, Germany, Austria, Czechoslovakia, China and Russia. These might also be called lager-porters, since most are lagered in the style of American lager-ale (i.e. **Yuengling Porter** from that Pennsylvania brewery), see I-4. Typical formula for this type includes 3% 80 to 120 L caramel malt, plus 12-18% (!) black malt, plus 1% dextrin malt, and 17% high dried malt, such as Munich or amber. Incidentally, **Anchor Porter** was (may still be) brewed with bottom yeast as a common beer (steam beer) when it was first brewed (1975).

Nugy (12) tells American brewers to aim their porter to over 13.5/1055, alcohol over 4/5%, and color over 20 lovibond (or SRM), very dark amber, 7 or more. His recipes at 12/1048, 13/1053, and 15/1062 call for up to 20% dark caramel malt, 2% black malt, 20% corn grits and 0.25gm/l of licorice in the kettle, and about 50 bitterness. Licorice and Molasses were commonly employed in old-time porters and stouts.

Wolfgang Kunze (7a) gives us "Deutscher Porter" 18/1074, brewed from 7-10% black patent malt, plus caramel malt, and 51 i.b.u., as an East German brew. It seems porter is very popular in the Communist bloc (where and when available).

PROFILES

beer's gravity OP/OG	alcohol ww/vv	beer's AE/BG	hops ibu	color/SRM
Black Hook Porter				
12.4/1050	4/5	2.8/1011	35	8.5
Boulder Porter				
13.5/1055	4.2/5.3	3.4/1013	45	9.5
Hale's Celebration Porter				
11.7/1047	3.8/4.8	2.6/1011	38	8.5
Samuel Smith Taddy Porter (E)				
12/1048	4.1/5.1	2.2/1009	n	8.5
Sierra Nevada Porter				
14/1057	4.6/5.8	3/1012	34	9
1887 American Porter				
18/1074	4.9/6.1	6.7/1027	54	n
1899 American Porter				
13.3/1054	4.2/5.3	3/1012	56	n

NOTES

III-8. Black Beer: Dry Stouts, Double, Imperial and Sweet Stouts

As the beer style known as porter came to be brewed stronger the name stout-porter came into use indicating stronger porter. "Stout" was followed by double stout and Imperial stout for even stronger beer. By mid-nineteenth century, the stout-porter had become the Irishman's national brew, and of these, **Guinness** the most famous. Today, stouts are usually fairly strong beers with rich maltiness and intense hoppy flavors. Original extract 13.5/1055 and over, alcohol content over 4.4/5.4%, apparent extract around 2.8/1011, bitterness over 25 i.b.u., and color 8.5-9.5/35-70SRM. Ingredients include pale English 2-row barley malt, plus dark caramel malt (80-120L), chocolate and black malt along with sugar, in some cases, and also sometimes including flaked barley. Infusion mash British style, and forced attenuation (ferment) to reduce apparent extract or beer gravity. As stated earlier, there is an overlap between this category and porter, which is entirely proper as the brewer is the final arbitor in such matters, and which accounts for the fact that few breweries have managed to brew both styles successfuly.

Guinness advertising indicates something like the following as their formulation: Pale 2-row ale malt, plus 9% each of flaked barley and very dark roast barley, in a two-step infusion mash (1-hour at 148-151°F/64.5-66°C). Bullion bittering and Golding aromatic hops to 50 i.b.u.

Wahl's (15) American or single stout: 17/1070, 76 bitterness, and Nugy (12) offers an American stout suggestion in his 1937 edition: not less than 15/1062 gravity, alcohol over 5%, and color at 40 lovibond (SRM).

Hough, *et al* (6) gives us some **Guinness** parameters at their many breweries and contract breweries at 10-11.5/1040-46, alcohol 3.5-4.1/ 4.4-5.1, and 55-62 bitterness. This is no doubt for **Draught Guinness** as the **Guinness Extra Stout** is stronger than that, and renowned across the planet for that very reason (see profile below).

SWEET STOUT, MILK STOUT AND OATMEAL STOUT

As for **sweet stout**, an English variation, Hough gives us **Mackeson** parameters at 11.1-11.9/1044-48, fairly low alcohol 2.9- 3/3.7-3.8, and 27-31 bitterness. Sweet stout is usually much lower in alcohol and original gravity than dry stout, 11-12/1044- 48, and color very dark amber, 7-8.5/ 30-39SRM. This makes sweet stout to be brewed more in the range of porter (see category III- 7), but with higher apparent extract (3.2/1013 and over) due to a greater residual sweetness from sugars, dextrins, or even added lactose. These are also called oatmeal or milk stouts depending on their makeup. These latter incorporate oats or flaked oats and sometimes lactose in their formula.

DOUBLE STOUT AND IMPERIAL STOUT

Imperial stouts may be expected to reach barleywine dimensions (18 Plato/1074). Richardson's 1805 "porter" is certainly a stout-porter at 20/1078, apparent extract 5.8/1023 with molasses in the kettle, and a very respectable 5.9/7.4% alcohol content.

Wahl's (15) double stout 19/1076, 109 bu, Imperial stout 22.5/1092; 120 bitterness and Russian Imperial export stout over 25/1105 at *140* bitterness. Wow! Of course the bitterness level projected above is our estimate, and could work out to as much as 30% less bitterness, but that's still rather hefty.

PROFILES

beer's gravity OP/OG	alcohol ww/vv	beer's AE/BG	hops ibu	color/SRM

1982 ABC Extra Stout (Singapore — bottle conditioned)

| 15.9/1065 | 5.4/6.8 | 3.3/1013 | 49.5 | 9.5 |

1884 Barclay & Perkins Double Stout (in E)

| 18.8/1077 | 6/7.5 | 4/1016 | 125 | n |

Belikin Stout (Belize)

| 13.9/1057 | 4.4/5.5 | 3.4/1013 | 28.5 | 9 |

1987 Boulder Christmas Stout

| 16/1066 | 5/6.3 | 4/1016 | 45+ | 9.5 |

BridgePort Stout

| 13.5/1054 | 4.5/5.6 | 2.7/1011 | 35 | 9 |

Grant's Imperial Stout

| 17/1070 | 5.6/7.1 | 3.4/1014 | 70 | 9.5 |

1982 Grant's Russian Imperial Stout

| 19.5/1080 | 6.5/8.1 | 3.9/1016 | 80 | 9.5 |

Guinness Extra Stout (E)

| 13.2/1052 | 4.4/5.5 | 2.8/1011 | 50 | 9.5 |

1901 Guinness Extra Stout (in Ireland)

| 18.2/1075 | 6.3/7.9 | 3.4/1014 | 90 | n |

Hillsdale Terminator

| 14.1/1058 | 4.1/5.1 | 3.6/1014 | 60 | 9 |

Mackeson Stout (Eng-sweet stout)

| 11.5/1046 | 3/3.8 | 4.3/1017 | 29 | 8.5 |

Samuel Smith Imperial Stout (E)

| 17.6/1072 | 6/7.6 | n | 9 | |

Samuel Smith Oatmeal Stout (E)

| 12/1048 | 3.6/4.5 | 3.4/1014 | n | 8.5 |

Sierra Nevada Stout

| 16/1066 | 5.1/6.4 | 3.8/1015 | 44 | 9.5 |

1900 American Stout

| 18.2/1075 | 5.4/6.7 | 5.5/1022 | 85 | n |

NOTES

III-9. Dark Beers: Celebration Ales, Barleywine Ale, Strong Country Ales, Lager Beers and Belgian Triples

These beers are characterized by rich malty flavor and good bitterness, but that characteristic is often masked by the maltiness and the characteristic alcohol taste, which can be quite intense, since most of them have over 6/7.5% alcohol content. Original extract over 18/1072. Other parameters are not sharply defined, but most of these beers are relatively dark (6.5-8.5/20-40SRM), quite hoppy, and have a hefty beer gravity or apparent extract. These ale beers have only two things in common: their high original extract and top ferment (for bottom fermented types see doppelbock category III-4, except that Samichlaus Dark may be bottom fermented. We have it here because it tastes and acts more like a barleywine than a doppelbock. We can be arbitrary at times.) Ingredients include variously British 2-row ale malt, dark malts including caramel, amber, brown, chocolate and black malts plus roast barley, torrified barley or wheat (popped like popcorn at high temperatures), and sugar, molasses, or anything else that the brewer fancies.

The name *barleywine* is a recent one, because these ales were called "strong" ales in the good old days. Richardson's 1805 strong Burton ale (below), and another at 27.8/1117 gravity, 6.2/7.8 alcohol, and apparent gravity of the beer at 12.9/1052, rather sweet it would seem, sweet and dark! If those were "strong," he offers an "ale" at 21.8/1090, and 5/6.3% alcohol, with a beer or apparent gravity at 9.7/1039. These high beer gravities indicate poor malting and mashing techniques prevalent at the time, although our Burton profile (below) shows a stunning alcohol content. Richardson's figures do not indicate alcohol, but are gravity readings of wort (original extract) and beer (apparent extract), allow one to calculate the alcohol content of the finished beer, and in the profile below we were able to calculate bitterness as well.

BELGIAN TRIPLES AND BARLEYWINE STRENGTH ALES

The Belgians also make barleywine strength (over 7.2 degree Belg) ales and these are sometimes called "triples" in that country, but the actual definition of triple remains unclear even by Jackson (7a,b,c). Some Belgians of that strength appear below.

PROFILES

beer's gravity OP/OG	alcohol ww/vv	beer's AE/BG	hops ibu	color/SRM
Affligem Triple (B)				
17.6/1072	6.3/8	3/1012	n	5.5
7.2 Belg				
1975 **Anchor Old Foghorn**				
25/1105	7/8.9	8.1/1032	32	7
1987 **BridgePort Old Nucklehead** (seasonal Christmas)				
22.5/1092	7.1/8.9	6/1024	55	7.5
1864 **Dortmunder Adambier** (in Germany in 1897, age 33yrs)				
26.4/1111	7.4/9.2	8.8/1035	n	n
Gouden Carolus ML (B)				
19/1078	5.6/7.0	5.6/1022	n	7
6.1 Belg				
Hoegaarden Gran Cru (B)				
18/1074	6/7.5	4/1016	n	3.5
7.4 Belg				
MacAndrews (Scotland)				
17.6/1072	5.6/7.0	4.2/1016	n	6

PROFILES

beer's gravity OP/OG	alcohol ww/vv	beer's AE/BG	hops ibu	color/SRM

1986 Pacific Crest Snow Cap Ale (seasonal-Christmas)

| 18/1074 | 5.6/7 | 4.6/1018 | 53 | 6.5 |

1987 Pacific Crest Snow Cap Ale (seasonal-Christmas)

| 18/1074 | 5.6/7 | 4.6/1018 | 46 | 6.5 |

Saison Special (B)

| 19/1078/ | 7.2/9.1 | 2.2/1009 | n | 6 |
| 7.8 Belg | | | | |

1987 Samichlaus dark (Swiss-seasonal, winter)

| 28.7/1122 | 12/14.9 | .14/1000.5 | n | 7 |
| | | | | deep ruby color |

Sierra Nevada Big Foot Barleywine Style Ale (seasonal spring)

| 24.8/1102 | 8.4/10.6 | 4.6/1019 | 80 | 7 |

Thomas Hardy's Ale (E)

| 29.9/1127 | 6.4/8.6 | 17.1/1070 | 100 | 7 |

Toison D'or(B)

| 19/1078 | 6.8/8.6 | 4/1012 | n | 3.5 |
| 7.8 Belg | | | | |

Traquair House Ale (Scot)

| 19/1078 | 8.8/11 | 2.7/1011 | n | 7.5 |

Young's Old Nick (E)

| 20.5/1084 | 5.8/7.3 | 7/1028 | n | 7 |

1889 Worthington Burton (E)

| 21.5/1088 | 7.9/9.8 | 7.5/1030 | 100 | n |

1805 Burton strong ale (Richardson)

| 26.2/1110 | 9.6/12 | 3.2/1013 | 83 | n |

NOTES

NOTES

IV. WHEAT AND MISCELLANEOUS BEERS

6 categories – 34 profiles.

Profile code: Specific beers are listed with their original gravity in degrees Plato (OP) and in British gravity form (OG); alcohol content wt/vol; AE Plato/AG gravity; bitterness; and color 1-10/SRM. For example:

Spaten Club-Weisse (WG)
| 12.5/1050 | 4.1/5.1 | 2.5/1010 | 14 | 4 |

Translation: original gravity 12.5-Plato/or gravity 1050: alcohol 4.1% by weight/or 5.1% by volume: apparent extract 2.5- Plato/or gravity 1010: bitterness 14 b.u.: color 4 (1-10 scale). No SRM is noted, as that spec is unknown. An "n" in any other space indicates we also do not have that particular information spec on the beer.

COLOR DEFINITIONS

Color 1-10 scale:		SRM*
0	water	0
1-1.5	light straw	1-2.5
1.5-2	pale straw	2.5-3.5
2-3.5	dark straw	3.5-5.5
3.5-4.5	light amber	5.5-10
4.5-5.5	pale amber	10-18
5.5-6.5	dark amber or copper	18-26
6.5-8.5	very dark amber "dark"	26-40
8.5-10	"black"	40 & up

*SRM = Standard Research Method degree, roughly equivalent to the old lovibond degree, and is used by the ASBC, (American Society of Brewing Chemists). In this system color is noted as degree SRM. The Europeans use a unit called "EBC (European Brewery Congress) degree." This is variable, but sometimes:
1 degree EBC = 2.65 degree SRM, less 1.2.
1 degree SRM = 0.375 EBC degree, plus 0.46.

IV-1. Wheat Beers: Bavarian White Beers

South German style wheat beer (weizenbier) is top fermented in the usual fashion, but with a special yeast strain, which imparts a very distinctive taste. Weizen beers are made from 40-75% wheat, plus the usual malted barley and, in some cases, dark and roasted wheat or other roasted malts. Most are pale, or very pale, although this style also supports dark wheat beers (dunkel) and even "weizen bock" styles. The Bavarian style has special, almost clove-like, taste which may be mild to noticeable. Fewer hops are used and the alcohol content is medium. The head is quite thick, creamy and long lasting, due to the extra protein in wheat. Hefe-weizen is real-ale style, fermented in the bottle or keg, with yeast present. These latter have 10% krausen (freshly fermenting beer) added at bottling, plus isinglass finings, and a dosage of bottom yeast. Alcohol content 3.6-4.5/4.5-5.7%. Original extract 12-15/1048-61 (over 16/1066 in the "weizenbocks"). Apparent extract 2.3-2.8/1009-11. Bitterness 13-17. Color 2.5-4/3-8SRM, or darker, in the case of "dunkelweizens."

DUNKELWEIZEN

These are dark versions of the, usually pale, weizens described above, color 6.5-8.5/26-40SRM.

WEIZENBOCK

These are strong or "bock" versions over 16/1066 gravity, and stronger in alcohol (over 6/7.5%). See III-4 for further information on what constitutes "bock" parameters. Don't forget the 40-60% wheat malt, and darker color inherent in the type.

PROFILES

beer's gravity OP/OG	alcohol ww/vv	beer's AE/BG	hops ibu	color/SRM
Ayinger Export Weissbier (WG)				
12.3/1049	4/5.1	2.6/1010	12.8	4
1981 **Ayinger Export Weissbier** (WG)				
12.7/1051	4.1/5.2	2.5/1010	10.5	4
Ayinger Hefe-Weizen (WG)				
12.3/1049	4.1/5.2	2.4/1010	11.5	3
Ayinger Ur-Weizen (dunkel-WG)				
13/1052	4.1/5.1	3.2/1013	13.6	4.5
Hibernia Dunkel Weizen				
13/1052	3.9/4.9	3.6/1014	20	6

PROFILES

Oberdorfer or Sailer Weisse (same beer — WG)
    13.2/1053   3.9/4.9   3.9/1015   n   2.5
Paulaner Altbayerisches Weissbier (WG)
    12.9/1052   4.3/5.3   2.7/1011 18.5   4
1888 Schramm Weizenbock
    17.9/1074   4.5/5.6   6.8/1027 20   n
Spaten Club-Weisse (WG)
    12.5/1050   4.1/5.1   2.5/1010 14   4

NOTES

IV-2. Wheat Beers: North German Wheat Beers

These are low in alcohol (under 4/5%), pale, and often with just a hint of tartness in their makeup. Wheat content from 30- 75% of the total.

BERLINER WEISSE

The Berliner Weisse style is almost an appellation, since it can only be brewed in Berlin. **Berliner Weisse**, is very tart, with a hefty (20%) *lactobacillus* segment in its yeast, and is usually consumed with a shot of "schuss" — sweet raspberry or woodruff syrup. These are also low in hops (bitterness 5-15), and very pale (2-3/2-4-SRM).

GRAETZER BEER

Graetz beer is of low gravity and strongly hopped, and with ⅔-smoked highly roasted wheat malt, and ⅓ pale barley malt. Original extract 7.5-8.5/1030-34, from a single temperature infusion mash. Bitterness 50 i.b.u., German hops.

PROFILES

beer's gravity OP/OG	alcohol ww/vv	beer's AE/BG	hops ibu	color/SRM
Berliner Kindl Weisse				
7.5/1030	2.5/3.1	1.5/1006	4	3
1895 Berliner Weisse				
10.3/1041	3.5/4.4	1.9/1007	5	n

NOTES

IV-3. Wheat Beers: New American Wheat Beers

This has become what amounts to a separate style. It is certain that not all American wheat beers will match a German profile. American wheat beers may be anything that the brewer desires. Tom Baune (Hart Brewing, Kalama WA) has done much to work various wheat malts into some of his beers, and seems to have developed a "Northwest" style (**Pyramid Wheaten**) for himself, and Portland's **Widmer Weizen** is certainly not a German "weizen," having more in common with **Pyramid Wheaten** than any German wheat beer we've sampled. Given the nature of wheat malts available to American brewers, the results are almost certain to be quite different than their European counterparts. There are really no parameters for this beer style as yet, and there is obviously no reason why this new wheat style could not be made as a dark beer, or even bottom fermented.

The *Berliner weissbier* style (IV-2) was once made in this country, and is very tart with a *lactobacillus* segment in its yeast. Wahl (6) gives us an *American weissbeer* with pale malt and corn grits, but no wheat (!) at 27.5 i.b.u., and the 20% *lactobaccillus* infested yeast.

PROFILES

beer's gravity OP/OG	alcohol ww/vv	beer's AE/BG	hops ibu	color/SRM
August Schell Weiss				
11.5/1046	3.6/4.5	3/1012	n	3
Grant's White Bear Wheat Beer				
11/1044	3.5/4.4	2.6/1010	20	3
Pyramid Wheaten				
10/1040	3.2/4.0	2.3/1008	15	3.5
1986 **Pyramid Dark Wheaten Ale**				
12.5/1050	4/5	2.9/1012	20	7

PROFILES

beer's gravity OP/OG	alcohol ww/vv	beer's AE/BG	hops ibu	color/SRM
Widmer Weizen				
11/1044	3.5/4.4	2.1/1008	18	4.5
1900 American Weissbeer				
9.3/1037	2.8/3.6	2.5/1010	27	n

NOTES

IV-4. Wheat Beers: Belgian Wheat & Lambic Beers (Lambeek)

Belgian beers represent what is probably the grandest array of exotic beers on the planet. Belgian wheats are mostly tart, but some are sweet-sour, and others only faintly tart. The lambics are the strangest, for they are fermented by natural yeasts (*Brettanomyces*) rather than by cultured yeasts. Most Belgian beers have additional bacterial contributions to their flavor profiles, but the lambics are a step beyond that. Moreover the hops used in the Lambic style are always a year old, and the wheat *unmalted* winter wheat! Alcohol content ranges from 3-5/3.8-6.3%.

GUEUZE

Blending a fresh lambic with an old, creates a second fermentation, and producesg a Gueuze. See profiles below. These are sharp tart beers at low pH 3.2-3.5, with 90-100% apparent attenuation or ferment.

FARO

A sweetened, sometimes diluted lambic beer, usually less than a year old. No samples here.

LOUVAIN WHITE BEERS

Louvain beers are from 50% unmalted raw wheat, and 50% green (unkilned) malt, plus some raw oats, resulting in complicated mashing cycles of up to 17-hours (4). The Hoegaardse Whit type: **Hoegaarden White** has a tart acidic palate and original extract 10.5-11/1042-44. According to Jackson (7a) this style has recently been revived in Belgium with formulations that have even included figs!

PROFILES

OE Belgian degree listed below OG

beer's gravity OP/OG	alcohol ww/vv	beer's AE/BG	hops ibu	color/SRM
Hoegaarden White (B)				
12/1048	3.8/4.8	2.8/1011	n	1.5
4.8 Belg				
Lindeman's Gueuze (B)				
12.9/1052	4.5/5.7	1/1004	26.9	6
5.2 Belg				
1871 Lambic (B)				
17.2/1069	6.4/8	15.3/1061	28	n
6.9 Belg				

NOTES

IV-5. Miscellaneous Beers: Specialty, Zuur, Herbal and Smoke Flavored Beers

This section includes any beer which will not fit in any of the previous categories, such as smoked beer, Belgian *zuur* (lactic acid) beer, and beers with honey, molasses or herbal flavorings. These beers are of a very unique nature. There are no "standards" here.

RAUCHBIER

Bamberg in Germany is famous for its smoked beers, from malts which have been dried with beechwood chips, during which time the smoke penetrates the malt, and when the beer is made it too is infused with this character. There is also a smoked wheat style known as *Graetzer* (IV-2), which is very rare.

STEINBIER

This beertype has recently been revived in Germany. Porous stones are superheated and lowered into the beer wort, causing that to boil, and then they are removed, and when the resulting beer has begun to ferment, and the stones are cool, they are again lowered into the beer, where the yeast ferments the strong sugars crystalized on the stones. The result is a delicious, rare and somewhat smokey beer.

FLANDERS BROWN ALE

A **zuur** or lactic acid style brew, these are sharply refreshing and faintly to strongly tart, dry and assertive lactic character. See **Bios** profile (below). Their unique yeast and warm fermentations lead to a fruity, spicy complexity. Ingredients include brown malt, blended with caramel, and Lambic beer blended in.

PROFILES

beer's gravity OP/OG	alcohol ww/vv	beer's AE/BG	hops ibu	color/SRM
Anchor Our Special Ale, 1987 (*spiced* ale-Christmas-seasonal)				
16.5/1068	5.1/6.4	4.3/1017	55	7.5
Bios Copper Ale1 (*zuur* beer — B)				
13.5/1054	5/6.3	1.5/1006	n	7
1985 **Grant's Winter Ale** (Christmas) (*herbal* ale):				
15.2/1061	5.3/6.6	2.6/1010	n	6
1987 **Hillsdale Kris Kringle** (seasonal-Christmas-*spiced* ale):				
14.1/1057	3.2/4	6.5/1026	48	5.5
Kaiserdom Rauchbier (*smoked* beer, WG-Bav):				
12.7/1051	3.9/5	3.2/1013	25.5	8.5
Rodenbach Gran Cru (*zuur* beer, B):				
13.5/1054	5/6.3	1.5/1006	n	5.5

NOTES

IV-6. Miscellaneous Beers: Specialty Fruit Flavored Beers

Specialty fruit beers are those where the fruit addition is a significant factor in taste or marketing of the beer. The kriek and framboise are Belgian *zuur* or *lambic* ales with cherries or raspberries. These beers are of a unique nature. Some fruit beers are flavored with "essences" at the end of the process, while others have real fruit added at the end of the kettle boil. Readers should try them, and draw their own conclusions. There are no "standards" here.

KRIEK AND FRAMBOISE

Blending cherries or raspberries with fresh Belgian *Lambic* beer causes a second fermentation and produces a **Kriek** or **Framboise**. See profiles of **Lindeman's** beers below.

PROFILES

beer's gravity OP/OG	alcohol ww/vv	beer's AE/BG	hops ibu	color/SRM
Hillsdale Ruby Tuesday (*raspberry* beer):				
9.8/1039	3/3.8	2.6/1010	25	pale pink
Lindeman's Framboise (B)				
15.9/1064	3.1/3.9	8.5/1034	n	pink
Lindeman's Kriek (B)				
13.2/1053	4.9/6.1	1.4/1005	24.5	maroon
Liefman's Frambozen (B)				
14/1057	4.7/5.9	2.7/1011	21	6.5
Liefman's Kriek (B)				
13.1/1052	6.2/7.8	2.4/1010	14	6
Morte Subite Kriek (B)				
12.8/1051	4.1/5.2	3/1012	n	6
Portage Bay Raspberry Pale Ale (Can)				
11.5/1046	3.6/4.6	2.9/1011	12	4
1970 U.S. citrus flavored malt liquor				
16.6/1068	4.1/5.2	6.7/1026	5	n/2.3

NOTES

COLOR DEFINITIONS

Color 1-10 scale:		SRM*
0	water	0
1-1.5	light straw	1-2.5
1.5-2	pale straw	2.5-3.5
2-3.5	dark straw	3.5-5.5
3.5-4.5	light amber	5.5-10
4.5-5.5	pale amber	10-18
5.5-6.5	dark amber or copper	18-26
6.5-8.5	very dark amber "dark"	26-40
8.5-10	"black"	40 & up

*SRM = Standard Research Method degree, roughly equivalent to the old lovibond degree, and is used by the ASBC, (American Society of Brewing Chemists). In this system color is noted as degree SRM. The Europeans use a unit called "EBC (European Brewery Congress) degree." This is variable, but sometimes:
1 degree EBC = 2.65 degree SRM, less 1.2.
1 degree SRM = 0.375 EBC degree, plus 0.46.

Profile code: Specific beers are listed with their original gravity in degrees Plato (OP) and in British gravity form (OG); alcohol content wt/vol; AE Plato/AG gravity; bitterness; and color 1-10/SRM. For example:

Lindeman's Kriek
    13.2/1053   4.9/6.1   1.4/1005   24.5   maroon

Translation: original gravity 13.2 Plato/or gravity 1053; alcohol 4.1% by weight/or 6.1% by volume: apparent extract 1.4Plato/or gravity 1005: bitterness 24.5 b.u.: color maroon. An "n" in one of the spaces indicates we do not have that particular information spec on the beer.

NOTES

PART III — BEER TASTING
JUST FOR THE FUN OF IT
by Fred Eckhardt & Itsuo Takita

This section is based on our original booklet, Beer Tasting and Evaluation for the Amateur, © 1977, and 1980, and published by ABIS, Portland, Oregon.

INTRODUCTION TO PART THREE

When we first published our little beer tasting pamphlet in 1977, little had been written on the subject of beer tasting. To be sure there was some literature pertaining to the specialized tasting requirements of the brewing industry; but most of that was not really applicable to our purpose. Since that time a number of books have been written to educate folks about the wonderful world of beer, most notably those from Michael Jackson (7a,7b,7c) the London beer critic. In fact today, there actually are beer writers; people earning a significant portion of their income writing about beer. Wine writers have been plying their trade for decades now, but beer writing is still in its infancy. It is important to remember that it may be beer and wine enthusiasts who will keep the new prohibitionist movement at bay. The more we enjoy the benefits of these wonderful old alcohol beverages, the more knowledge we have about them, the better the likelihood that we will be able to defend ourselves against those who accuse us of so-called "drug abuse."

Our purpose is the same now as it was in 1977. It is to encourage people to think about beer and beer tasting in the same way wine enthusiasts (I hate the word "connoisseur") think about wine and wine tasting. We want to suggest procedures to follow in recreational beer tastings, for the comparative evaluation of beer.

We have not changed our original tasting procedure, nor the form we recommend using for that purpose. For the actual tasting procedures we have leaned heavily on wine tasting literature, notably Amerine and Roessler (16) (see bibliographical references at the end of this section). The most pertinent beer tasting literature we have found, has been published by the American Homebrewers Association (30,32), Charles Finkle (24), Howard Hillman (26), our own previous work (23), and also a dissertation by Michael Weiner (33), now out of print. Some brewery literature was quite valuable, notably Meilgaard's "Flavor Wheel" (19), Compton (20), Lewis (28), and chapters in DeClerck (21), and Hough *et al* (27).

● ● ●

Praise not a beer until it has been drunk.
old Viking Proverb

Judge the Beer in the Glass
from Amerine and Roessler

PART THREE – CHAPTER ONE
COMPARATIVE TASTING OF BEER

There has been a flood of new beers entering the American market. These are both import beers and those from the many new microbreweries and pub breweries which have started up around the country. One of the more interesting side effects is that there are now beer tastings done in the way wine lovers have been doing for many years.

The *Los Angeles Times* has conducted annual beer tastings for several years now, and here in Portland, Oregon, the beer tastings in the last year have probably outnumbered, or at least matched, the wine tastings! This has certainly had the effect (here) of increasing the numbers of new beers introduced in the city, thus (presumeably) improving the selection available. That selection has increased from 57 new beers in 1984 to 107 in 1985, 121 in 1986, and 108 in 1987. This competition on the market has had a salutory effect on beer in Portland. It is not only that we have more beers being introduced here, but also that we have had *better* tasting beers being brought in, or produced here in Portland. Our brewery population has increased from one brewery in 1983 to seven (1988), and now there's even a "brewery district," four breweries within walking distance (1km), possibly the only such district outside of Europe. The story is repeated variously in California, New England, and Wisconsin. Other areas are following along, too; the movement is spreading.

Comparative tasting of beers has been an important factor in building Portland's beer livability. Comparative tasting of beer is what this section is all about. We hope the information here will aid people to evaluate their own and commercial beers. We believe the result will be to improve the quality of beer available all over the U.S.

THE CARE AND SERVING OF BEER

Beer is an extremely fragile and perishable product. It begins to deteriorate immediately as it is packaged. The great European beer that is so distinctive in the city of its origin becomes bland and less tasteful when found in this country. Why is this? Simply put, beer is easily damaged by movement, light, vibration, age, and exposure to air. Breweries must make heroic efforts to ensure that their beer arrives at its destination in the best possible condition. For those reasons, beer is usually pasteurized, heavily filtered, and often treated with various enzymes and chemicals to keep it fresh for the customer. When this is done, the product is called "export" beer, and the taste profile is always blander and less interesting.

Almost all American breweries make their beer to "export" standards, so their beer tastes much the same no matter where you find it. The Europeans usually give the "export" treatment only to that beer which is actually to be shipped to other places. Often, their regular beer, as found in their local taverns and pubs, tastes much better. That is what the tourist remembers about the beer.

The more intense flavor profile of good local European beer (hoppier and/or maltier) coupled with different alcohol definitions prevalent in Europe, determines that a tourist who has just returned from Germany or England, will be absolutely certain that German or English beer is very much stronger than our beer in this country. When you couple the fact about alcohol strength to the stronger taste profile of European beer, you can get a real opinionated beer drinker who just "knows" that European beer is much stronger than ours. As you can see from our catalog of styles (Part Two), there is no great difference between the alcohol content of European beers and those of our own.

THE NATURE OF BEER IN THE BOTTLE

Most beer drinkers have little understanding of the perishable nature of beer. This is also true of the people who market beer, the wholesalers and the retailers. Beer should be transported carefully and kept refrigerated during transport and storage. Needless to say, that is not always managed.

HOW TO FIND FRESH BEER

Commercial beer is best when it is fresh (it is best consumed within three to six weeks of bottling) because it begins to deteriorate immediately on leaving the brewery. All commercial breweries date their beer, usually in code, often on, or in the back of, the label; and nearly always on the case (sometimes not coded). The consumer should buy only the freshest beer in stock. It helps to know something about brewery dating codes on bottled and canned beer.

BREWERY DATING CODES

The most common date code (square or rectangular labels) notes the months along the sides of the label (see Anheuser Busch box). The indication is in the form of notches at the edge of the label. The notch codes can be quite complex, a coded entry telling those "in the know" the exact date and time the beer was bottled, see the **Budweiser** code (box). Another common date code system notes the months clock-like in a clockwise pattern around the label (round labels), i.e., 1:00 # January, 2:00 # February, 11:00 # November, etc.

Europeans and Asians sometimes date code their beer with a six figure date. The day, month, year (e.g., 16 12 88 = 16 December 1988) may be on the case or the reverse side of the label (viewed through the beer) as is the case with Thai **Singha**.

THE JULIAN DATE CODE

Some breweries actually print the date across the label, on the bottom of the can, or on the reverse of the label (viewed through the bottle from behind). This date is usually a "Julian" date, a 3-digit number which is the the number of the day in the year. January 1st is day number 001, and December 31 is 365 (or 366). The last digit of the year will precede or follow that number, and perhaps other information will be coded there too. **Heileman** and **Pabst** use the Julian code, **Coors** enters an uncoded "pull date," such as Jul 22. The beer should be drunk before that date. The sooner the better.

ANHEUSER BUSCH CODE

The **Budweiser** label is square, and the months are noted January through June on the left side (J-F-M-A-M-J), and July through December on the right side (J-A-S-O-N-D). The brew-month is notched, 1 notch is the 1st through the 15th, and 2 notches for the 16th through the 31st. At the bottom of the label, there is space for another month, but the notches there indicate the year, 1-notch odd years, 2-notches even years.

The brewery also uses the Julian date, in a 10 character code impressed onto the bottle (near the bottom) or the can (on the bottom). Here is a code on a bottle I found recently:

0888S36286

088 the Julian day March, 29. The next character "8" is the last digit of the year 1988, which changes the date (leap year) to March 28, 1988. The letter "S" is for the brewery, St. Louis, MO. The last 5 numbers indicate the time of bottling within 15-minutes, but I don't have the key to that. The bottle was in my hands on May 5, so the beer was a little over 5-weeks old, and should have been drunk quickly — it was.

FRESHNESS

Freshness is even more important for imported beers because of the great distance they must travel to your door. As we have said, beer does not travel well, it is best at the brewery. Imported beers often lack freshness codes, and when they do exist they usually need a special key which may or may not be available to the importer or wholesaler, and which in any case is seldom shared with store owners or customers. It wouldn't hurt if the reader were to try to get this information from the wholesaler or importer of a favored beer. Do whatever it takes to get fresh samples of your favorites. Of course some breweries do use the Julian date or variations of that, and maybe you can figure out which is which. I found some Julian dated Australian **Fosters Lager** on the shelf near where I live. The stuff was over six months old!

SEDIMENT

Some beers are **supposed** to have sediment. These are good quality bottle-conditioned beers, and the sediment is the result of a ferment in the bottle. The bottle ferment creates carbon dioxide gas, which gives the beer its condition (carbonation) and the sediment comes from the expired yeast cells. Beers that are conditioned by a ferment in their serving container are called "real ales." Real ales are certain English and English-style ales, stouts, porters, German wheat beers, and a number of fine Belgian ales. They are even made here in the U.S.: California's **Sierra Nevada** Ales, and Colorado's **Boulder Brewery's** ales among others. In such bottle conditioned (German: hefe-) beers, if there is no sediment the beer may actually be flat.

Lager beers are almost never finished in this manner, and sediment is fairly rare. There are many times when sediment will be found to be quite damaging to the beer. This can happen to beers which have been on the shelf for an overly long time. When the bottle is turned over, the light fluffy sediment will resemble "snow." That may be a pretty sight, but the taste is totally dreadful. It tastes quite like a skunk smells, and indeed it is called "skunky." If you find such a beer do not buy it, but take it to the proprieter, and ask that he remove it from his shelves. Most shopkeepers have no idea at all about the shelf life of beer, but they should listen to your complaints, especially after they taste the beer.

Tulip Champagne   Brandy   Flute

Figure 1 — Glass styles for beer tasting (courtesy Libby Glasware)

THE BEER GLASS

I prefer to drink my beer from a large brandy snifter. Occasionally, for recreational drinking, I like a stone mug, sometimes chilled in the refrigerator, but never frozen in the freezer.

When I evaluate a beer carefully, for my notes or files, I use the Champagne tulip. For evaluation purposes, beer must be presented in a glass. The Champagne tulip (9-oz size) has a deep or hollow stem which will trap bubbles for slow release of the aroma and bouquet. The narrow area at the lip of the glass serves to concentrate the aroma and bouquet, in the same way that it is designed to do for Champagne. The brandy snifter, and the standard wine tulip glass are also satisfactory for similar reasons, however neither has a well to trap bubbles. For my beer tasting classes I use small (5-oz) brandy snifters.

"BEER CLEAN" GLASSES

Glasses for a beer tasting should be especially clean, if the head of the beer is not to be ruined. This level of cleanliness is called "beer clean" in the tavern industry. They offer these directions: (22)

1. Wash beer glasses carefully with a good detergent.

2. Do not use soap, but rinse thoroughly.

3. Do not dry wipe glasses. Permit them to air dry upside down in a dish rack or such. If water droplets cling to the glass, or if spots show while drying, the glass is not clean. A "beer clean" glass will air-dry crystal clean with no spots whatever.

4. Rinse the glass with fresh cold water just before serving the beer. It is best to serve the beer in a wet glass. This will prevent bubbles clinging to the glass after you pour the beer. If you didn't rinse the glass, and bubbles do cling to the glass, tap it or tap the glass bottom on the table. The bubbles will pop to the surface of the beer.

SERVING THE BEER

We Americans prefer our beer chilled to about 38°F (3°C), or even colder. This is much too cold to enjoy the full flavor of good beer. U.S. breweries generally recommend their beer to be served at 42-44°F (5-7°C). Germans drink theirs at about 50°F (10°C), while the English prefer their beer at cellar temperature, about 55-60°F (13-16°C). I don't think you can judge beer properly if it is served cooler than 45-50°F. This is certainly true at beer judgings or competitions, but the beer buff who compares beers at home for fun should do so at whatever temperature he or she wishes. Bear in mind that the flavor of the beer is not released until it has been warmed, if not in the glass, then in your mouth.

Beer is tastiest when it is served with a collar or head, and should be drawn or poured with that objective in mind. The only exception to this is cask conditioned British-style real ale draught which should be drawn to completely fill the glass. The head on this type of beer tops the glass!

THE GOOD SOUND OF BEER

Just as the bubbling noise of a pot simmering on the stove can enhance our anticipation of the coming dining experience, so the gurgling of a beer being poured in a glass, and other related sounds, has an important effect on our appreciation of that beverage. The beer tasting instructions from the Weihenstephan Brewing School in Munich tell us all five senses are to be used: "to sight it must ring clear as a bell, it must snap in the ear, feel pleasantly sticky between the fingers, smell fresh and tempting and taste heavenly. The foam must be sprightly, upstanding and crackling; it is as important as the bead on old ale or wine." There is a reason to *Listen to Your Beer!*

● ● ●

Figure 2— Other glass styles are also suitable for beer presentation (Durobor of Belgium)

PART THREE –
CHAPTER TWO
USING THE TASTING FORM

It has been argued that we don't really have a grasp of what constitutes good beer flavor. Professor Lewis (28) points out that "good beer flavor has become synonymous with the 'absence of flavor faults'...which falls well short of defining flavor." "What is needed," he says, "is a language that is as widely understood as possible, i.e., a simple one." Lewis argues that flavor is a balance of various elements at levels of both intensity and quality.

We feel that the flavor of beer is a combination of sweet, bitter, and sour tastes with the olfactory stimulus of odors, *plus* the tactile sensation of the beer touching various parts of the mouth. We've compiled a short glossary of these terms, as they apply to beer tasting. (Appendix). This is a glossary of positive taste elements, mostly those factors which contribute to the flavor of good beer. The critical evaluation and judging of beer for beer competitions is not the objective of this dissertation. Our purpose is rather to educate beer enthusiasts to evaluate commercial or privately made beer for their own enjoyment. Most beer drinkers are unable to identify the endearing qualities of their favorite beer, but they can nearly always find what they don't like about a given beer.

EVALUATION AND SCORING

There are many ways to evaluate beer (or wine). We are more interested in quality judgement, where the beer is judged on certain qualities with regard to its comparative ranking and value in the way that wine is judged. There are many ways to score such judgements and evaluations to make them meaningful, but two are more important. We can score by evaluating the beer on a point basis, as in wine judging, using a 20-point system (or 30, 50, or 100 points). Alternately we can judge on a plus-minus, like-dislike basis (e.g. +5 to -5). This latter would create what is called a *flavor profile*.

The beer scoring system which we proposed in our first edition, 1977 (23), and which we still think is superior, is based on the so-called *Davis score card* developed at the University of California Davis, School of Enology, for rating their experimental wines and also for training students in the sensory evaluation of wines. Much of the literature on sensory evaluation (16,27,30,31,32,33) stresses the importance of the pre-tasting examination. We fully agree. Sight and smell are of critical importance to the evaluation of any beverage, but especially to that of beer. Accordingly, this procedure is weighted to give 35% of the score to sight and smell.

THE TWENTY POINT SCALE

Although the 20-point scale is not new, it has been rejected by the major homebrew judging

groups — American Homebrewers Association
(AHA) and the Home Wine and Beer Trade
Association (HWBTA — in favor of a more com-
plicated 50-point scale.

For our purposes, i.e., recreational judging and
evaluating beer in the home, the simple 20-point
scale described below is easier to use. Our rating
system is divided into four departments: 1 & 2)
before tasting (sight and smell), 3), *in the mouth*
(taste, touch and olfactory), and 4), *post tasting*
(summation). We have weighted these departments
— wine tasting style — at 3/20, 4/20, 10/20, and
3/20.

PROCEDURE FOR USING THE
20-POINT SCORE SHEET

Note: Many of the tasting terms used here are
defined in the glossary (appendix). It is important
to understand the meaning of these descriptive
terms. Comments on the beer should be restricted
to the words in the glossary and the vocabulary
presented in the following descriptions. Your com-
mentary will be much more meaningful if this is
done. A plus (+) or minus (−) after some terms are
to guide you in evaluating a particular quality.

Judge the beer in the glass.

Feel free to use half-points.

The score sheet is divided into four segments: appearance; odor; taste and in-mouth feel; and
general impression. These are each judged
separately and the results added together for the
total score of that beer.

1. APPEARANCE – PRE-TASTING VISUAL EXAMINATION.

a. **Examine the bottle for sediment.** Certain beers should throw a sediment, others may not. A light sediment in bottle conditioned beers is proper and commendable. Minus (–) for heavy sediment, which is never proper. Commercial (usually micro-brewed) lagers and filtered ales may occasionally show a very thin sediment (–), but **export** class beers should not have even the faintest touch of sediment. Sediment in an **export** beer is a major flaw, and probably indicates old (too old) beer. **Export** style commercial beer must be completely non-sedimentary and brilliant.

b. **Pour the beer**. Pour 4-6 oz (120-180ml) of the beer into the glass. Pour in such a manner as to produce a collar, or head, about 3/4-inch (2cm) thick. With some commercial beers, this may mean turning the bottle upside down while pouring straight down the center of the glass. Do not fill the glass more than about ⅔ full. Leave at least a fourth of the glass' volume empty. Sedimented bottle conditioned beers and ales may need to be decanted carefully, so as to avoid disturbing the sediment. It should also be noted that some ales, stouts, and porters may have less foam, due to their minimal carbonation, as expected with many beers of that class. On the other hand some beers are expected to have more foam. Wheat beers, especially the hefe-weizen (hefe- bottle conditioned) beers, and some others, notably Belgian, are famous for their heavy foam.

If the beer gushed it should probably be discarded as unacceptable, unless it is clear that the beer has been mistreated, and that is the reason for gushing.

Note: The quality of both the visual and, to a lesser extent, the aromatic constituents, depends on the way the beer is poured. Improper pouring of the beer will result in either too much or too little head (collar) — not necessarily the beer's fault; but to its detriment in the visual and olfactory examination. A good head is necessary, both to the beauty of the presentation, and because the aroma and bouquet are released most effectively during the period immediately after pouring the beer.

c. **Quickly sniff the beer.** Volatile aromatics (e.g., hop nose from dry hopping) do not linger, and must be caught right after the beer is poured (see

---

COLOR DEFINITIONS

Color 1-10 scale:		SRM*
0	water	0
1-1.5	light straw	1-2.5
1.5-2	pale straw	2.5-3.5
2-3.5	dark straw	3.5-5.5
3.5-4.5	light amber	5.5-10
4.5-5.5	pale amber	10-18
5.5-6.5	dark amber or copper	18-26
6.5-8.5	very dark amber "dark"	26-40
8.5-10	"black"	40 & up

*SRM = Standard Research Method degree, roughly equivalent to the old lovibond degree, and is used by the ASBC, (American Society of Brewing Chemists). In this system color is noted as degree SRM. The Europeans use a unit called "EBC (European Brewery Congress) degree." This is variable, but sometimes:
1 degree EBC = 2.65 degree SRM, less 1.2.
1 degree SRM = 0.375 EBC degree, plus 0.46.

no. 2 below). Take 2- 3 quick whiffs, swirl, and take several more short sniffs.

d. **Examine the beer in the glass.** For a period of one minute, examine the beer for color, clarity, gas release, and head stability. The color should be correct for the beer type. You may note the color on the form, either by name or by our number (1-10):

Gas release — the bubbles should be *small*, compact, and continue to be released during the visual and olfactory examination. If the room is quiet enough, you might put your ear to the glass and listen for the sound of the foam disintegration, which should be a pleasing series of clicks, not a steady buzz.

Head condition and stability — note whether the head is correct for the beer. (Remember, not all beer is supposed to have a good thick collar, while steam beer, weissbeer, wheat beers and some home brews may exhibit a very thick collar). After a one-minute period, the collapse of the head should be less than 50% (+), if more than that (−). If the head is lacking (−), or there is too much foam (even after carefully decanting) — as in some homebrews (−), adjust your award accordingly.

TOTAL AWARD — APPEARANCE: Maximum 3 points. Minimum acceptable 1, Ordinary sound beer 2.

2. ODOR — PRE-TASTING OLFACTORY EXAMINATION.

Note: This is done while you are waiting for the head collapse, and in conjunction with the visual examination of the beer in the glass. See note earlier about aromatics immediately after the beer has been poured.

Sniff the beer again — take a good strong sniff, paying special attention to the hop nose, the aroma, the bouquet, noting especially any off-odors that may be present:

Aroma — this is the (non-hop) odor of the beer. Aroma is the character of the raw materials in the beer, unaffected by the ferment. Aroma is readily identified in most low-hopped American-type beers (**Budweiser, Millers, Molson,** etc.). Dark lagers and brown ales generally have greater aromatic intensities from the roasted malts used in their manufacture.

Bouquet — this comes from the odors of the fermented elements of the beer. Bavarian wheat beers have a special bouquet and character of their own, a plus (+), but usually a flaw (−) when found in other beer types. Belgian beers sometimes have an intense bouquet from the special yeast strains used to produce them. This is a plus (+) in those beers, but might be considered a flaw (−) in other beers.

Hop nose — this is the hop aroma of the beer. Beer should have a distinct or neutral hop character, and you should be able to detect it. The hop nose should be correct for the beer type. English hops in English-type beers (Bullion, Goldings, Fuggles, etc. — an excellent example of this is in the nose of **Young's Special London Ale**, which is dry-hopped with East Kent Golding hops). Several American ales have this special hop effect from dry-hopping, notably **Anchor Liberty Ale** and **Sierra Nevada Celebration Ale**. Some traditional European lagers (made to purity law standards) achieve the same thing by special treatment of the hops, which has the effect of adding essential oils. Some other brewers will simply add those hop oils direct at the end of ferment. The effect is similar to that of dry hopping: an enhancement of the hop nose, which is apparent immediately when the bottle is opened. The hop nose in this case is expected to be that of Continental hops, such as Hallertauer, Saazer, Tettnang, Spalt or Northern Brewer.

Draft beers will rarely exhibit this characteristic hop nose unless they have been prepared "real ale" style, which usually includes dry hopping in the cask or keg.

American style lagers, dark lagers, bock beers, etc., will have less hop character than their European counterparts, but many American ales will have *more* hop nose than their English counterparts. You should always be able to detect *some* hop character in pale beers, even the American style. Note however, that wheat beers usually have very little hop character. The **hop nose** of a beer might be intense, impressive, pronounced, noticeable, mild, or lacking. Score (+) or (−) in accordance with the beer-type. For example, an American lager (I-1 or I-2) might have only a mild hop nose, but a premium beer should have at least a noticeable hop nose. There should be no noticeable off-odors either. If any negative odors are detected, such as medicinal, oxidized, musty, acetic, yeasty, sulfide, sour or infected, (see appendix glossary for definitions), score (−) or 0 — unacceptable. Other more pleasing side-odors might include fruity, nutty, malty, and some fermenting odors. If you feel these latter side-odors contribute to the beer, do not deduct, but if they do not contribute, deduct (-1, -1 1/2).

TOTAL AWARD – AROMA AND BOUQUET: maximum 4, minimum acceptable 1, ordinary sound beer 2.

Note – The **pre-tasting** examination *must* show at least 1 point each (#1 and #2 above), or the beer should be deemed unacceptable, and discarded.

3. TASTE IN THE MOUTH
After you have completed the above, you may taste-sample the beer.

TASTING PROCEDURE

Take a good sip (about 1-tablespoon, 15ml) of the beer. Swirl and slosh it around your mouth. Finish off the initial taste by opening your mouth a little and inhaling a bit of air (wine tasters call this "swizzling") to aerate the beer and excite the olfactory region at the base of your nose. It is the combination of olfactory, taste, and tactile examination that gives us the impression of "flavors."

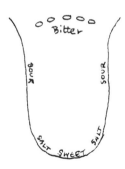

Figure 3 – The four taste areas of the tongue

Take a smaller sip to record the basic taste areas of your tongue: the sweet, salt, sour, and bitter areas (see illustration), *in order*. Try to keep them separate so as to identify those tastes in that order.

Take another small sip for mouth-feel; pass some of the beer along the inside of your lower lip (to check astringency, but which should not cause your inside lip to swell). As you can see, this is both a taste and tactile (touch) procedure and, as the beer warms in your mouth, it becomes olfactory as well.

It will be necessary to swirl the glass, from time to time, to rejuvinate the release of aromatic elements. Finally, take another small sip, and evaluate the aftertaste, or tail. Wine judges traditionally do not swallow wine, other than a tiny drop; beer judges, on the other hand, nearly always swallow the beer they have tasted. Taste again, and again, as necessary, and in the same manner, to evaluate the total taste-in-the-mouth.

After all that, you should clear your mouth with a sip of water, perhaps accompanied by bread, cracker, or pretzel. (Cheese or butter on the lips may damage the head of the beer, and alter the receptivity of the glass).

This is one unit: score 0-10. This award is determined without breaking down the elements of the beer. Score the in- mouth beer as a whole, balanced, unit. The key to success in tasting is experience. You should be able to project an image of the "classic" profile of that beer style in your mind, then compare that with what you are judging. This profile is from the following seven areas. Do not consider odor or appearance, as these have already been evaluated separately (above). Concern yourself with only the following:

Hop quality — there should be a good varietal taste, smell, and aftertaste: pronounced, moderate or lacking, as expected of the beer type.

Hop intensity — should be correct for the beer type.

Sweet/dry balance — is the sweet/dry (non-sweet) balance correct for the beer. Tartness (see next) is sometimes mistaken for dryness, especially in low alcohol beverages such as beer.

Beer character — this is the sum of non-hop, non-sweet/dry characteristics of the beer. These should be readily identified: malt and grain character, the nuances generated by the malting and roasting techniques, from the specialty malts used in the beer, may be noticeable. The taste and flavor profile should be correct for type. Beer character includes tart or non-tart rather than sourness from intense acidity, although there are beers (weissbeers and Belgian zuur beers) that do exhibit a lactic tartness. Lactic tartness is acceptable in some beer-types, but an acetic or vinegary effect would be sour, and such beer must always be rejected.

Excessive malt or tannic bitterness or astringency would also be negative, and even hop bitterness, where harshly noticeable, might be negative.

Any noticeable taste, such as a special "brewery" taste might be classified as neutral, negative (−) or even positive (+), depending on your impressions, and on the beer style in question.

Aftertaste or tail — swallow a little of the very first tasting of the beer to evaluate the aftertaste or tail. Some hop character might linger, along with other characteristics. This normal lingering taste should be pleasant and disappear fairly soon. The aftertaste might be classified as pleasant (+), disappears rapidly or lingers not unpleasantly (+)

or (−) depending on balance. It might be harsh or rough and include clinging tastes (−). Additional off-tastes might include lingering tartness, astringency, mustiness, acetic, while still others could include clinging bitteness from hops or grains, which would always be negative, and perhaps even unacceptable.

Body and Palatefullness — body is the alcohol character and richness of the beer. Palatefullness is the "feel" of the beer in the mouth, dependent on the condition (carbonation and CO_2 content), fullness, neutral alcohol qualities, and the structure of the beer. **Body and palatefullness** may be dry, vinous, neutral, sweet, bland, full-bodied, thin, smooth, rough, watery, and correct or not correct for beer type.

Flavor balance — How is the beer "supposed" to taste, compared with how it *does* taste — is it correct for ale, lager, stout, etc. Flavors and off-flavors may include malty, spicy, astringent, yeasty, sulfide, medicinal, oxidized, light struck, metallic, sour, bitter, salty, etc. Positive or negative may influence your award here. This is the balanced taste, and aftertaste, of the beer.

TOTAL AWARD — TASTE IN THE MOUTH: maximum 10, minimum 5 (less than 5 would be unacceptable in commercial beer), 5 poor, 6 fair, 7 ordinary good beer, 8 fine, 9 superior, 10 ideal or perfect.

Feel free to use half points.

4. GENERAL QUALITY

This is the combined response. Not to be used to adjust the score of the beer, but rather as a separate and distinct part of the award. According to

Amerine and Roessler (16) "It is the memorableness of the character of the (beer), or its lasting come-hither appeal."
Score: Impressive 3, good 2, fair 1, lacking 0. Ordinary sound beer 1 or 2.

TOTAL SCORE OF THE BEER: A beer must meet *ALL* minimums to be commercially acceptable. Unacceptable means the sample is *NOT COMMERCIALLY ACCEPTABLE.*

It is highly unlikely that any commercial beer would actually be "unacceptable." What is more likely (if you thought a given beer *was* unacceptable) would be that the beer was damaged after it left the brewery, or that a bad batch has escaped from the brewery's care without being discovered. Your own dislike of a particular beer-type should not be used as grounds to discard the beer.

RATINGS – TOTAL SCORE:
19-20 Great, ideal. Up to 5% of all beers. This is "world class" or gold medal class.
17-18 Superior beer. 10% of all beers, silver medal class.
15-16 Fine beer. 15% of all beer bronze medal class.
13-14 Good beer, 25% of all beers.
12 Ordinary beer.
9-11 Fair commercial beer.
8 Poor beer, but commercially acceptable.
under 8, or under minimums in any of the first three scored areas: **Unacceptable.**

● ● ●

HOMEBREW JUDGING

If the reader wishes to become a judge in homebrew competitions, he or she should contact the home beer supplier nearest them (yellow pages) for the name of a local homebrew club, or write either of the following national organizations that sponsor training of homebrew judges. Write:

American Homebrewers Association, P.O. Box 287, Boulder CO 80306-0287
and/or

Home Wine and Beer Trade Association, 604 N Miller Rd, Valrico FL 33594.

● ● ●

PART THREE – CHAPTER THREE
TRAINING YOURSELF

This is not a training program to qualify you as a beer judge, but rather a preparatory course to calibrate your palate for your own tasting enjoyment.

First, spend about two weeks familiarizing yourself with the best selling U.S. beers (type I-2, North American Standard). Start with **Budweiser**. Later add the other nationals (**Millers, Coors, Strohs**, etc.). Then add the "regular" local beers to your list. Taste five or six samples of each beer you select.

1. Taste before you eat. Your taste buds are better in the morning, but this is not really a good time for recreational beer tasting, and I question the wisdom of drinking any alcohol beverage in the morning unless required by your job as a professional brewer. I do my own tastings in the evening (before dinner), usually at about 4:30 or 5pm.

2. Use the procedures outlined earlier for each tasting. For training purposes try to score **Budweiser** at around 12-13 points. Do this even if you think American standard is boring beer. Let us not forget that Bud, the current best-selling U.S.

beer, is an excellent example of the brewer's art. Of course it is very possible the reader has a strong preference for another national, say **Coors** or **Strohs**, and if that is so, then by all means use that beer. Any good American beer in a brown bottle will do for these tastings. For reasons that will become clear, the brown bottle is a "must." My recommendation is **Budweiser** because it is made locally (or nearly so) across most of the U.S., and because it is clean tasting, well made, nearly always fresh, and universally available in this country. It is clearly the standard from which to judge others of its type.

The purpose of these preliminary tastings is establish a point of reference for all your tastings — in other words to calibrate your palate. Repeat the tastings, aiming at the 12-13 point score, but do not try to remember your previous awards, "Judge the beer in the glass." Don't doctor your score to comply with the desired end, but do each tasting separately. When you reach a point of reference with **Budweiser**, you are ready to work around it by trying different beers, and then as you become more skilled, work to establish a point of reference with a popular International (type I-7) import such as **Heinekens**. You might try for 13-15 points with **Heinekens**. Run the same program with whatever other beers you wish, working up or down from **Bud** or **Heinekens** in those two beer classes. When you have tried a variety of good commercial beers, you are ready for the following training sequence.

Buy two bottles of **Budweiser** with the same date code, try to get bottles that are directly fresh from the factory, and which have not been in the display case, exposed to fluorescent light. You may have to get the manager to open a new case for these samples. Place one of the samples in a sunny window, and leave it stand for a week or two. Store the other sample in the refrigerator. After the exposure to sunshine, place the sample in the refrigerator, alongside the other, to chill for the tasting. Do not make any attempt to remember which is which. Now have someone serve them to you side-by-side in a blind tasting. Which one is the light-struck (skunky) sample? Try the same test on **Millers**. You might be surprised to find that **Millers** in a clear glass bottle tastes less damaged than did the **Bud**. That is because of the special treatment **Millers** gives its beer to minimise the effects of light. Both these breweries claim "natural" treatment, but only one reacts "naturally" to light.

Next, while waiting for the above beers to "ripen," prepare further tests as follows: (mark them #1-#7)

1. Remove the cap from one bottle and leave it open in the fridge for a week. When that is ready, prepare the following seven additional samples as well. De-carbonate each sample by pouring it back and forth to rid it of CO_2, and then doctor them as follows. The de-carbonation process will make the beers flat, and thus easier to compare with the first sample (oxidized). Be sure to thoroughly dissolve each additive into the beer.

2. Add a teaspoon of winemaker's citric or tartaric acid, (tart).

3. Add a teaspoon of household sugar, (sweet).

4. Pour a fourth of the beer out and replace it with water, (weak).

5. Buy a small sampling of hop pellets from the nearest home beermaking shop. Add about a tablespoon of pellets to a small teapot, and add about a pint of boiling water, bring to a boil, simmer about 5-minutes, and allow to cool. Do this

ahead of time. When ready, pour out about a fifth of the beer, and replace it with hop tea, (hop bitterness).

6. Pour out an ounce of beer and replace that with an ounce of vodka, (strong).

7. This one is decarbonated only, as a control or "undoctored" sample.

The above, rather primitively doctored samples, will go a long way towards educating your palate. You should do the actual tastings "blind" (poured by a friend) and poured into coffee cups so you can't tell any possible color changes in the various beers you have ruined.

The above training program could just as well be undertaken by a group. You might work some other educational ventures into your training program, such as a three-way (2 of 1, and 1 of the other) taste between bottled and canned samples of the same beer, or between the regular brand and its cheaper sister (i.e., **Budweiser** and **Busch**), or between the regular brand and the "premium" beer (**Budwieser** and **Michelob**). See if you can detect a "house" or "brewery" character between them. Then conduct a blind tasting between several beers you have worked with, such as the top five nationals, and see if you can identify them.

● ● ●

Opposite is our Beer Evaluation and Score Form. The reader should feel free to reproduce and use this form for beer tastings but not for resale purposes.

BEER EVALUATION AND SCORE FORM

Beer name _____ Beer type/class _____

Beer identification data, and information (specific gravity of beer, etc.) _____

Color intensity (1-10) _____ Alcohol content _____

1. PRIOR TO TASTE
Appearance, head, condition, bubbles, proper color, clarity. **Score 0-3 (minimum 1, ordinary beer 2)**....

2. ODOR
Aroma (beer character) and bouquet (hop character). **Score 0-4 (minimum 1, ordinary beer 2)** ....

3. IN-MOUTH FEEL AND TASTE
Hop quality and intensity, sweet/dry balance, beer character, body and palatefulness, aftertaste, and overall flavor. **Score 0-10 (minimum 5, ordinary beer 7)** ....

4. AFTER TASTING
General quality and memorability. **Impressive 3, good 2, fair 1, lacking 0** ....

Your total score **(minimum acceptable 8)**..

Your comments about the beer (if any) _____

Remember, the beer is unacceptable if it does not meet all minimums.

BIBLIOGRAPHY OF SOURCE REFERENCES
– TASTING INFORMATION

(reference numbers are a continuation of
original bibliography in part one)

(16) Amerine, M.A., and Roessler, E.B., *Wines, Their Sensory Evaluation*, San Fransisco CA, 1976: W.H. Freeman & Co.

(17) Anderson, R.J., "Measurement and Description of Flavour," *Brewers' Guardian*, November 1983.

(18) Bengtsson, K., and Helm, E. "Principals of Taste Testing," *Wallerstein Laboratory Communications,* Dec. 1946, IX: 28, 171.

(19) Clapperton, J.F., Dalgliesh, C.E., and Meilgaard, M.. "Systematic Beer Flavor Terminology," *The Practical Brewer*, Second Ed., 1977: Madison WI, Master Brewers Association of the Americas, p433

(20) Compton, John, "Beer Quality and Taste Methodology," *The Practical Brewer*, Second Ed., 1977: Madison WI, Master Brewers Association of the Americas, p288.

(21) DeClerck, Jean, "Tasting Tests," *A Textbook of Brewing*, (translator Barton-Wright, Kathleen), v2, 1958: London, Chapman- Hall, Ltd., p632.

(22) *Draft Beer Facts and Trouble Guide* by Tap Right, Hackensack, NJ.

(23) Eckhardt, F., & Takita, I., *Beer Tasting and Evaluation for the Amateur*, Revised Ed., 1980: Portland OR, ABIS Publications.

(24) Finkel, Charles, "How to Give a Beer Tasting," *Alephenalia* 1982 edition, 1982: Merchant du Vin Corp, Seattle WA.

(25) "Glossary of Some Terms Used in the Sensory (panel) Evaluation of Foods and Beverages," *Food Technology*, 1959: XIII; 12, 733.

(26) Hillman, Howard, *The Gourmet Guide to Beer*, 1987: New York NY, Facts on File Publications.

(27) Hough, J.S., Briggs, D.E., Stephens, R., and Young, T.W., "Beer Flavour and Beer Quality," *Malting and Brewing Science*, Volume II, Second Ed., London 1982: Chapman-Hall.

(28) Lewis, M.J., "A Concept of Beer Flavor," *Brewer's Digest*: L,9; 56 (Sept 1975).

(29) Olshausen, Joern J., "The Psychology and Interpretation of Taste Tests," *Siebel Contributions,* Sept 1957; 35.

(30) Papazian, Charlie, "Beer Flavor Evaluation: Testing Yourself," *Zymurgy*, Spring 1986: 9;1,25., American Homebrewer's Association, PO Box 287, Boulder CO 80306.

● ● ●

*Additional bibliography, pp. 40-41.

APPENDIX

GLOSSARY OF POSITIVE OR NEUTRAL TASTE TERMS
Please read carefully

Alcoholic – a hot sometimes spicy sensation/flavor which, if noticeable, is usually negative, but barleywines and some doppelbocks have an alcohol character that contributes greatly to their goodness. An example of negative alcohol character may be found by adding a jigger of vodka to any American Standard beer, making the beer seem unbalanced.

Aroma – odors that originate from the ingredients used in the beer (see bouquet).

Belgian – having the special bacterial character of some Belgian beers. Positive in some beers, when that character has been designed into the beer, but negative in most beers. The Belgian **Orval** or **Chimay** ales are excellent examples of the fine qualities such a character can add to a beer.

Bitter – a taste. Quinine is bitter, hops are bitter in various degrees, pleasant or unpleasant. A number of compounds in beer can have bitter tastes, we usually distinguish hop bitterness, desirable (+), from non-hop bitterness, usually neutral or non- desirable. Note that even hop bitterness may be too intense for the beer type (–).

Body — fullness of flavor and mouthfeel — see also **palatefullness**.

Bouquet — odors that originate with the ferment (see aroma).

Brilliant — completely and totally free of suspended matter (+).

Butterscotch — see **diacetyl**.

Buttery — see **diacetyl**. Sometimes called butyric.

Caramel — burnt sugar or baked flavor (+) or (–). See also oxidized (negative term). May be perceived as molasses or licorice, but in a negative sense.

Carbonated — good in proper balance, but if the beer is gassy, i.e., the carbonation is excessive or very noticeable, or flat (lacking) it would be faulted.

Diacetyl — butterscotch, buttermilk, caramel or buttery. May be slightly positive or neutral, but usually is negative when there is a strong diacetyl character.

Dry — lack of sweetness, not to be confused with tart.

Fermenting (odor) — the mild odor of fermenting yeast: if very mild this may be acceptable in some bottle conditioned common beers and ales, but is totally unacceptable in commercial "export" type beers, such as lagers. See next.

Fresh — odor of young beer past the fermenting stage, see above. This may be acceptable, neutral, or negative, depending on the intensity, and the beer type.

Fruity — fruit-like character, may or may not be desirable, but would definitely be expected in a fruit beer. On the more or less negative side, this could be described as the fruitlike character of citrus, apple, banana, black current, melony, pear, raspberry, and strawberry, most of which would be undesirable, depending on beer-type and flavor intensity.

Herbal — having an herbaceous character from herbs used in its makeup which might, or might not, be negative, but would be required in some beers, e.g. a "dill" beer would need a "dill" character, a garlic beer would be expected to have some "garlic" taste, but neither should overwhelm. Of course, a non-herbal beer should have NO herbal character, and if it were detected, that would be a negative. See also **spicy**.

Honey — when this is lightly apparent, as in a beer with honey, it is positive, but it may also be negative.

Mature — properly matured beer. This term is most applicable to ales, weissbeers, and home brewed beers which can age (+). It should be noted that most commercial beers will simply get old.

Nutty — the mild and pleasant sherry odor which may or may not be desirable in beer (depending on intensity and beer type), but which would be neutral at best and negative at worst. May also be described as walnut, coconut, bean soupy, and almond as in marzipan.

Palatefullness — is the "feel" of the beer in the mouth, dependent on the condition (carbonation), fullness, neutral alcohol qualities, and the structure of the beer. Body and palatefullness may be dry, neutral, sweet, bland, vinous, full-bodied, thin, smooth, rough, watery, and correct or not correct for the beer type.

Satiating — filling or extra full. This is a positive characteristic in some barleywines and imperial stouts, but negative in pale lagers for example.

Spicy — an especially distinct spice aroma which would come from the use of spices in the beer. Such spices might include Coriander, ginger, cinnamon, nutmeg, allspice, pepper, and other spices found in some herbal beers, such as holiday ales. Needless to say, if the aroma (or taste) is more than slightly noticeable it is probably undesirable (see also herbal).

Sweet — positive in some beers, when expected in the beer-type, but negative sometimes, if it becomes too noticeable or when it is cloying or oversweet.

Tart — clean acidity, as in lactic acid, a rather pleasant tartness, not to be confused with dry or sour or acetic. An especially sought after quality in weissbeer and some Belgian zuur beers, but quite often negative when more than very slightly noticeable in some ales, and definitely negative in lagers of any kind. May be (−) or (+).

Vinous — a fusel or wine-like character, neutral at best, or even negative.

● ● ●

The above characteristics are more likely to be positive (+) or neutral, but a few might be considered negative (−) under some circumstances (see next).

GLOSSARY OF NEGATIVE TASTE TERMS
Please read carefully

NOTE: These characteristics are rarely found in commercial beers, but might be found in brewery beer, home made beer, and beer stored or packaged under defective circumstances. This is by no means a complete list of negative factors, but rather a few of those more likely to be encountered. These are nearly all negative aspects of beer.

Acetaldehyde — a natural fermentation by-product which is beneficial in very small quantities (6-8ppm). It is also a product of heat (as in sherry wine). In larger amounts it is quite deleterious: If it is noticeable it is unacceptable. **Acetaldehyde** shows up sooner in the blood of those who may be susceptible to alcohol abuse.

Acetic — vinegary, totally unacceptable in any beer (even Belgian).

Astringent — often perceived as a mouth-feel rather than a flavor ("mouth puckering"), and is usually the result of excessive tannin in the beer, mostly from grain husks, but sometimes from the hops as well, often noticed when pale beers are over-hopped.

Autolysed — rotting yeast, see also **yeasty**.

Burnt — bread crust, charred toast, roast barley, smokey.

Characterless — bland, empty, flavorless. See also **watery**.

Cidery — somewhat tart, but tartness with no body, as found in the old home brews of the Prohibition era. May not be always be negative, but usually so. Sometimes this effect is called (incorrectly) winey.

Clear — as opposed to **brilliant**. Definitely negative, but only slightly so. The character of having a very few suspended particles — possibly to an extremely faint, almost non-existent, haze. Nevertheless, a step down from **brilliant**.

Cloudy — having a light colloidal haze or yeast matter in suspension.

Cooked Vegetables — as in cooked cabbage, corn or broccoli, from sulfur compounds in the beer — a definite defect when noticeable. See also **DMS**.

DMS (dimethyl sulfide) — cooked corn, celery, parsnips, or even oysters. Sometimes found in beer as a "house character." When minimal this may be perceived as a positive aspect, but usually negative if it is noticeable.

Dull — definite colloidal haze — beer unacceptable unless this is clearly a result of refrigeration, or in a bottle conditioned beer that has been accidentally shaken before decanting.

Earthy — see **moldy, musty**.

Estery — Ethyl acetate, solvent-like, isoamyl acetate or banana-like. Ethyl hexanate or apple/anise-like. Negative if noticeable.

Flat — lacking in carbonation, negative if noticeable, but remember that "real ales" (cask conditioned draught beer) might be characterised by that name, but we still stand by our "negative if noticeable" standard. Real ales should not be tasted as "flat," (see next).

Gassy — excessive carbonation, fills the mouth with bubbles and prickly sensations, as soda pop, negative if noticeable. See also **flat**.

Grainy — graininess, sometimes noticeable in beers with high corn-adjunct usage, is not necessarily negative unless perceived as such. A delicate nuance of the taste balance in a beer.

Grassy — the flavor of freshly cut grass. Negative if noticeable.

Husky — from the malt husks in the malt. Negative if noticeable.

Light-struck — see **skunky**.

Medicinal — see **phenolic**.

Metallic — usually harsh and unpleasant as in the taste of iron, rusty water, coins, tinny, and inky. Unacceptable if noticeable.

Moldy — earthy or cellar taste, clearly evident and always unacceptable, usually fungal in nature. See also **musty** (next).

Musty — odor of old cellar, earth, some mushrooms, decaying newspapers, etc., unacceptable if noticeable.

Oxidized — can be stale with a cardboard or paper taste ($-$), sherry-like (see **acetaldehyde**) or winey and cidery ($-$), nutty (neutral), or even as overripe fruit or garbage.

Papery — initial stage of staling, as in stale bread, cardboard, old beer. See also **oxidized**.

Phenolic — having a medicinal character ($-$). Easily recognized, and nearly always unacceptable.

Rough — astringent or tactile, but not "bitter."

Salty — negative, if even slightly noticeable.

Skunky — having the characteristic smell of a skunk, from exposing the beer to light which alters some of the hop character negatively, a sulfur compound. This can be a powerful flavor, but is frequently subtle and easily confused with hoppiness, especially when found in green bottled European lagers. To sample this at its worst place a bottle of *Corona* in the sun for a few days, then chill and compare with a fresh (from the case) sample of the same beer. Beer in green or clear glass bottles is susceptible. Amber or brown bottles are the best protection for beer, although they will also become light struck when left in the sun for a few days.

Sour — acidic; when tart becomes sour it may be negative. See also **acetic**.

Sulfury — odor of sulfur or hydrogen sulfide (H_2S — the odor of rotten eggs).

Thick — usually negative, from being viscous, but might also be used to mean **satiating** or filling.

Watery — thin, seemingly diluted, not to be confused with low calorie beer, which is designed to be watery. Low alcohol beer can also be watery, but shouldn't. Watery low alcohol beer is, by its very nature, defective.

Woody — as in seasoned wood, uncut wood, not oak as in a beer that has been aged in oak (some Belgians).

Yeasty — strong fermentation or yeast odor, undesirable in every case (–).

● ● ●

Bud Light
   7.8/1031   2.6/3.3   1.7/1007   10 (est.)   2

An almost tasteless example of the brewer's
manufacture (certainly not brewer's art!), but one
with more character (higher apparent extract, but
less alcohol) than arch-rival **Millers Lite**.

● ● ●

Erratum — from pages 48-49

For example, a bottle of **Bud Light** tells us it contains 108 calories, 9 grams carbohydrate, and 1.1 grams protein.

carbohydrate cals = 9 × 4.1		=	37.0
protein cals	= 1.1 × 5.65	=	6.2
total non-alcohol cals		=	43.2
subtract from 108 cals		=	64.8

divide by 7.1 = 9.13 grams alcohol

divide by 3.55 cl (12 oz.) = 2.57% by weight, which is 3.23% by volume.

The unfermented or real extract is 1.1 gm protein + 9 gm carbohydrate = 10.1 gm real extract in the beer.

Divide 10.1 by 3.55 cl = percent of real extract (RE): 10.1/3.55 = RE 2.85%.

But we need the apparent extract (AE) (also known as the beer gravity), and the formula for that, when the real extract is known, is:

AE = RE − (alcohol by wt × 0.46), therefore AE = 2.85 − (2.57 × 0.46) = 1.67 = 1006.5 gravity.

However, we want to know the original gravity of this beer, so multiply alcohol percent (wt) by 2.4:

$$2.4 \times 2.57 = 6.17$$

this is the gravity drop during the ferment. Add this to the beer extract (AE):

6.17 + 1.67 = 7.84 original gravity (OG) in degrees Plato, which is 1031.4 original specific gravity.

The beer's profile, then, is

AFTERWORD

This has taken a lot longer than I imagined it would, and so an afterword is necessary. As I mentioned earlier, the book has had a life of its own, no wonder then that it has not seen fit to finish itself on any schedule I might have set for it.

Meanwhile, I don't think I have given much credit to Michael Jackson in my acknowledgments, yet it is apparent to me that I would not have written this particular tome were it not for him. Michael's writings and his encouragement of my own efforts have been an inspiration to me since we first met at the American Homebrewer's Conference in the Chautauqua Hall in Boulder, Colorado, in 1980. I want to acknowledge that debt. We have had many great beers together (and not a little wine) since then. I hope there will be many more of each in the years to come.

●

As time goes on, it becomes obvious that we drinkers are becoming an endangered species. My friend Tom Burns, Detroit brewing lawyer, insists that the anti-alcohol lobby has/is invented/inventing a disease that the health care industry can pay for. He's right, the anti-alcohol lobby promotes the idea that there is no such thing as "responsible drinking." How are we to fight this? What do we say when our schools teach our children (two thirds of whom will grow up to drink): "just say No to drugs and alcohol." I asked an eight-year-old boy on my swim team, "What would you do if you were President?" His chilling answer, "I'd outlaw drugs and alcohol." Nice kid, his father works for the Portland Blitz-Weinhard Brewery.

More important (and more likely) is the possibility that as this boy gets older, he will note that his father works for a brewery, and perhaps even drinks the stuff. He may then wonder if 1) his father is a criminal, or 2), has someone been lying to him about alcohol? And if that is so, then perhaps they are also lying about drugs. That possibility chills me to the marrow, because that's how much of the drug trafficking began in the late 60's. The youth of that era found that the marijuana of the time was obviously not leading to heroin use, and they began to question the whole government line about drugs.

We need to educate young people, two-thirds of whom will drink when they grow up, about drinking responsibly. We need to teach enjoyment of drinking for the good taste, and the great contributions alcohol has made to our civilization, rather than making it a rite of passage for adolescents who seek effect rather than enjoyment. The Europeans have far fewer problems with alcohol than we do, because they learn to enjoy it from childhood on. Our children are not allowed to learn to deal with alcohol gradually, they are thrust into it by their peers, not under the supervision of adults. No wonder they have problems coping.

Only one drinker in ten develops problems in

alcohol control, and yes, I am aware of how severe those problems can be. At age 63, I have watched not a few good friends in some of their bouts with alcohol, and sadly, many of them are now unable to drink any alcoholic beverage at all.

It might have been different with some, had they been given information about the proper use of alcohol, instead of being thrown to the mercy of their peers for this important education. I remember my peers had nothing more in mind, for me, than to see if they could get me drunk and perhaps sick. They thought that was what they were supposed to do, both for themselves and for me. Since there is no way for us to legally train our young to manage their alcohol, they are left to their own devices. And as Tom Burns points out: "there is no reason to be moderate about it, if it is illegal to do it in the first place." Our young people need better guidance from their elders and unless we provide it for them, the problem of alcoholism will only get worse — not better.

The last prohibition may have brought on the Great Depression of 1929. We should all remember that alcohol consumption in the United States is not only legal, but it has a long and honorable history. There is nothing illegal or dishonorable about drinking alcohol, we need to keep that in mind.

In the interest of giving some guidance in these matters, let me offer some suggestions for you, which may help keep your alcohol use under some level of positive control. Many of these suggestions are taken from Gene Ford's marvelous new book, *The Benefits of Moderate Drinking: Alcohol, Health & Society*, published in 1988 by the Wine Appreciation Guild, 155 Connecticut St., San Francisco CA 94108 ($14.95), a book which belongs in every beer lover's library. I drew many of the following conclusions after reading Mr. Ford's work.

Evidence abounds that a small amount of alcohol taken daily, in the form of beer and wine, exerts a positive influence on our good health. This amount is one or two beers a day, or a smaller amount of wine (3-6 ounces). Now some additional amount of beer and wine on a daily basis is also reasonable and perhaps also beneficial. This would be moderate drinking. Moderate drinking has been defined as about 20% less than your weight divided by 3, which is the number of ounces allowed daily in beer. Divide your weight by 9 and you find the number of ounces of wine which you can comfortably imbibe on a daily basis. On some occasions you may have more, and rarely you may find yourself somewhat inebriated. All well and good, but what is abuse? I can answer that one too: heavy drinking is imbibing over 6-oz a day of ethanol, which translates to about two six-packs a day. This can cause (if you continue over a long period of time) damage to your liver and other organs.

If, after reading the above, you feel you might have an alcohol problem, let me suggest that you start cutting back. Get control of your own affairs. Don't drink before late afternoon, unless work requires it, and certainly don't do it in the morning. Try to skip one day a week, try to get back to the moderate level, and stay there. Your drinking pattern became heavier very gradually, and very likely you can reverse it gradually, too. Not everyone needs to quit totally. I have many friends who have reversed their drinking pattern to a more sane and rational level, and who continue to enjoy the wonderful benefits of moderate drinking and the delights of good beer.

One more point, if you are abusive of yourself and others when you do drink, then alcohol is not for you. You should quit before you harm yourself or someone else. If you find yourself drinking only for effect, you should seek counseling. It is very important that you recognize the danger signals before it is too late. And of course, don't drink and drive, be especially careful about that.

I hope this finds you well, and in good health, and I hope that you and yours will continue to enjoy good beer. May you live another hundred years, and enjoy good beer each and every day of that long and prosperous life. Prosit!

Fred Eckhardt
Portland Oregon
August 31, 1989

● ● ●

The cartoon on the following page was drawn by Isaiah Stewart, a 15-year-old Vancouver, Washington High School student, and a promising young illustrator. This is his first commercial sale and I think it shows fine talent for a lad so young.
—f.e.

"OUR BEER LIST SIR."

INDEX OF BEER PROFILES

● ● ●

GENERAL INDEX

ORDER FORM

ABIS — Fred Eckhardt Communications
PO Box 546, Dept. E
Portland, OR 97207-0546 USA
Telephone: (503) 289-7596

Please send me the following publications by Fred Eckhardt:

☐ *Essentials of Beer Style* $14.95

☐ Data Diskette (IBM/ASCII 5¼", 360K) with a list of
  over 1000 current beers filed according to the
  Essentials of Beer Style categories, showing Beer,
  Country of Origin, and Style. $19.95

The following **ABIS** publications are kept in print:

☐ AB #6 Special Yeast Issue, 20 pp, updated 1984 $2.95
☐ AB #8 Steam Beer, Beer Design, Malting, 28 pp $2.95
☐ AB #9 Brew Calculations for Homebrewers, 32 pp $3.95
☐ AB #10 Swiss Beer, Hops, Yeast, Wheat Beer, 24 pp $2.95
☐ AB #11 Dortmund Lagers, Wheat Beers, Altbier, 28 pp $2.95
☐ AB #12 Hop Special Issue, 32 pp $3.95
☐ Mashing Notebook, notes on home mashing, recipes $2.95
☐ Sake, our original authentic recipe $2.95

All of our publications are available wholesale to dealers and beer clubs. Send for further information.

Sorry, we are not equipped to handle credit cards; your check is welcome.

Total Order ____

Postage & handling 15% (minimum order) ____

Total Amount Due ____

I can't wait 4-6 weeks for delivery; please rush my
order (1 week). I am adding $2 for this extra service ____

Please add additional postage if you live outside the USA.

Total Enclosed $_____   ☐ Check   ☐ Money Order

(Sorry, no billing and no credit cards.)

Name _____

Address _____

City _____ State _____ Zip _____

THE AMERICAN HOMEBREWERS ASSOCIATION

Join the Thousands of Homebrewers Who read *ZYMURGY*

ZYMURGY—A Magazine for Homebrewers and Beer Lovers

Learn What's new in Homebrewing Including:

- New Recipes • Product Reviews • Tips for Beginners
- New Brewing Techniques • Equipment and Ingredients
- Beer News • Beer History • And Much, Much More!

SATISFACTION GUARANTEED!

Published five times a year by the American Homebrewers Association, **ZYMURGY** is included with membership.

Mail This Coupon Today!

— — — — — — — — — — — — — — — — —

_____ ENCLOSED IS $21 FOR ONE FULL YEAR.

(CANADIAN/FOREIGN MEMBERSHIPS ARE $26 US)

_____ PLEASE CHARGE MY CREDIT CARD

OR CALL NOW FOR CREDIT CARD ORDER AT 303-447-0816

VISA _____ MC _____ EXP. DATE _____

CARD NO. _____

NAME _____

ADDRESS _____

CITY _____

STATE/PROVINCE_____

ZIP/POSTAL CODE_____ PHONE _____

Make Check to: Zymurgy, P.O. Box 287-E, Boulder, CO 80306-0287